WORKPLACE LEARNING & PERFORMANCE ROLES

The MANAGER
and the CHANGE
LEADER

WILLIAM J. ROTHWELL

A Self-Guided Job Aid With Assessments Based on
ASTD Models for Workplace Learning and Performance

Linking People,
Learning & Performance

Ordering information: Books published by the American Society for Training & Development can be ordered by calling 800.628.2783 or 703.683.8100, or via the Website at www.astd.org.

Library of Congress Catalog Card Number: 00-111206

ISBN: 1-56286-283-9

◢ TABLE OF CONTENTS

		Page

List of Tables and Figures v

Section 1   **Getting Started** 1
♦ What Is the Background of This Project 3
♦ What Does This Job Aid Contain, and How Do You Use It? 3

Section 2   **Defining the Roles** 5
♦ The Role of the Manager 7
— Definition of the Role 7
— Importance of the Role 7
— The Relationship Between This and Other Roles 7
— The Place of the Manager in the Human Performance
Improvement Process 8
— Competencies Associated With the Role of Manager 8
— Outputs Associated With the Role of Manager 11
— Who Performs the Role of Manager? .11
— When Do They Perform This Role? 18
— What Projects Do Managers of WLP Carry Out? 18
♦ The Role of the Change Leader 18
— Definition of the Role 18
— Importance of the Role 20
— The Relationship Between This and Other Roles 20
— The Place of the Change Leader in the Human Performance
Improvement Process 20
— Competencies Associated With the Role of Change Leader 20
— Outputs Associated With the Role of Change Leader 20
— Who Performs the Role of Change Leader? 23
— When Do They Perform This Role? 30
— What Projects Do Change Leaders Carry Out? 31

Section 3   **Enacting the Role of Manager** 33
♦ A Model of the Management Process 35
♦ Steps in the Management Process 46
— *Step 1:* Formulate a Vision of WLP for the Organization, Department, or Work
Group 46
— *Step 2:* Communicate the Vision to Others and Build Their Enthusiasm 52
— *Step 3:* Clarify the Goals and Objectives Necessary to Realize the Vision 56
— *Step 4:* Clarify the People, Data, and Things Necessary to Realize the Vision 58
— *Step 5:* Create and Implement an Action Plan to Align With
Organizational and HR Plans 60
— *Step 6:* Establish the Policy, Select and Develop People, Organize and
Schedule Work Processes, Assign Responsibility, and Lead the Work 63
— *Step 7:* Establish and Maintain a Work Climate That Is Conducive to
Realizing the Vision and Implementing the Action Plan 66

    — *Step 8:* Develop a Follow-Up and Monitoring System to Track Results
       Against Intentions 68

    — *Step 9:* Establish and Implement a Communication Strategy and Plan to
       Build Enthusiasm for WLP Initiatives 70

    — *Step 10:* Work With All Necessary Stakeholder Groups to Ensure
       Continuous Improvement of WLP Efforts 70

    ♦ Section Summary 73

Section 4   **Enacting the Role of Change Leader** 75

    ♦ Model of the Change Leadership Process 77

    ♦ Steps in the Change Leadership Process 84

    — *Step 1:* Identify the Stakeholders Who Stand to Gain From the Benefits of an
       Intervention 84

    — *Step 2:* Formulate a Strategy for Collecting the Results of the Intervention and
       Communicating Them to Key Stakeholders 85

    — *Step 3:* Resolve Conflicts That Arise During Interventions 87

    — *Step 4:* Communicate the Results to Excite Enthusiasm and Inspire Others About
       the Intervention 88

    ♦ Section Summary 89

Section 5   **Tools for Conducting Management and Change Leadership** 91

    ♦ Introduction to the Tools Section 93

Section 6   **Afterword** 111

    ♦ Why Is It Important to Master These Roles? 113

    ♦ How Does It Feel to Perform These Roles? 113

    ♦ What Should You Do Next? 113

Section 7   **Bibliography** 115

About the Author 121

LIST OF TABLES AND FIGURES

Section 2   **Table 2.1:** Competencies Associated with the Manager's Role .9

Table 2.2: Sample Outputs Associated with the Manager's Role 12

Table 2.3: Competencies Associated with the Change Leader's Role 21

Table 2.4: Sample Outputs Associated with the Change Leader's Role 23

Figure 2.1: The Human Performance Improvement Process Model for the Role of Manager 8

Figure 2.2. Worksheet to Organize Your Thinking on the Work Expectations of Your Organization for the Manager's Role 12

Figure 2.3: The Human Performance Improvement Process Model for the Role of Change Leader 20

Figure 2.4: Worksheet to Organize Your Thinking on the Work Expectations of Your Organization for the Change Leader's Role 24

Section 3   **Table 3.1:** Relationship Between the Management Process and the Competencies of the Manager of WLP 37

Figure 3.1: Model of Management of WLP 36

Figure 3.2: Step 1: Formulate a Vision of WLP for the Organization, Department, or Work Group 47

Figure 3.3: Assessment for Establishing a Vision for the WLP Department or Effort 49

Figure 3.4: Instrument for Assessing Stakeholder Agreement About a Vision for the WLP Department or Function 50

Figure 3.5: Step 2: Communicate the Vision to Others and Build Their Enthusiasm 53

Figure 3.6: Worksheet for Brainstorming Ways to Communicate the Vision of the WLP Effort and Build Enthusiasm for It 55

Figure 3.7: Step 3: Clarify the Goals and Objectives Necessary to Realize the Vision 57

Figure 3.8: Step 4: Clarify the People, Data, and Things Necessary to Realize the Vision 59

Figure 3.9: Step 5: Create and Implement an Action Plan and Align It with Organizational and HR Plans 61

Figure 3.10: Step 6: Establish the Policy, Select and Develop People, Organize and Schedule Work Processes, Assign Responsibility, and Lead the Work 64

Figure 3.11: Step 7: Establish and Maintain a Work Climate That Is Conducive to Realizing the Vision and Implementing the Action Plan 67

Figure 3.12: Step 8: Develop a Follow-Up and Monitoring System to Track Results Against Intentions 69

Figure 3.13: Step 9: Establish and Implement a Communication Strategy and Plan to Build Enthusiasm for WLP Initiatives .71

Figure 3.14: Step 10: Work With All Necessary Stakeholder Groups to Ensure Continuous Improvement of WLP Efforts 72

Section 4   **Table 4.1:** Relationship Between Change Leadership and the
Competencies of the Change Leader 78

Figure 4.1: Model of Change Leadership 78

Figure 4.2: Step 1: Identify the Stakeholders Who Stand to Gain
from the Benefits of an Intervention 85

Figure 4.3: Step 2: Formulate a Strategy for Collecting the Results
of the Intervention and Communicating Them to Key Stakeholders 86

Figure 4.4: Step 3: Resolve Conflicts That Arise During Interventions 87

Figure 4.5: Step 4: Communicate the Results to Excite Enthusiasm and
Inspire Others About the Intervention 89

Section 5   **Figure 5.1:** Worksheet to Guide the Management of WLP .94

Figure 5.2: Worksheet to Guide Change Leadership 106

SECTION 1	GETTING STARTED

 ♦ What Is the Background of This Project?

 ♦ What Does This Job Aid Contain, and How Do You Use It?

SECTION 2	DEFINING THE ROLES

SECTION 3	ENACTING THE ROLE OF MANAGER

SECTION 4	ENACTING THE ROLE OF CHANGE LEADER

SECTION 5	TOOLS FOR CONDUCTING MANAGEMENT AND CHANGE LEADERSHIP

SECTION 6	AFTERWORD

SECTION 7	BIBLIOGRAPHY

What Is the Background of This Project?

The Manager and the Change Leader is an outgrowth of *ASTD Models for Workplace Learning and Performance* (Rothwell, Sanders, and Soper, 1999). It is a self-study job aid for the workplace learning and performance (WLP) practitioner that describes the competencies essential to success in the WLP field and contains information about the practitioner's roles as manager of WLP and change leader. (Additional volumes in this ASTD series focus on the practitioner's other roles—analyst, evaluator, and intervention selector, designer and developer, and implementor.)

As in other self-study job aids in this series, the role should not be confused with job title. Just as the word *role* in the theater refers to the part that an actor plays, in WLP a role is a part that the practitioner plays in the human performance improvement (HPI) process. Following is a complete list of WLP roles (see also Rothwell, Sanders, and Soper, 1999, pages xv–xvii):

♦ The *manager* plans, organizes, schedules, and leads the work of individuals and groups to attain the desired results; facilitates the strategic plan; ensures that workplace learning and performance is aligned with organizational needs and plans; and ensures the accomplishment of the administrative requirements of the function.

♦ The *analyst* isolates and troubleshoots the causes of "human performance gaps" or identifies areas in need of improvement.

♦ The *intervention selector* chooses appropriate learning and performance interventions (that is, corrective actions), both in and out of the workplace, to address the causes of these performance gaps.

♦ The *intervention designer and developer* formulates learning and performance interventions that address these causes and complement similarly targeted interventions.

♦ The *intervention implementor* ensures that the interventions that have been selected are carried out in an effective and appropriate way and complements similarly targeted interventions. In this capacity, the intervention implementor may serve as, for example, administrator, instructor, organization development practitioner, career development specialist, process redesign consultant, workspace designer, compensation specialist, or facilitator.

♦ The *change leader* inspires the workforce to embrace the interventions implemented, creates a direction for the effort, and ensures that the interventions are continuously monitored and directed in ways that are consistent with stakeholders' desired results.

♦ The *evaluator* assesses the changes made, the actions taken, the results achieved, and the impact experienced, and apprises participants and stakeholders accordingly.

Note that throughout this book, the author sometimes distinguishes between department, function, or effort. A WLP department might include an HRD or training department or a performance improvement or performance enhancement department. A WLP function might be found within another department, such as marketing or management information systems. A WLP effort might be a specific project, such as the installation of a customer-improvement program or a management training program.

What Does This Job Aid Contain, and How Do You Use It?

The Manager and the Change Leader is a book designed to enhance your knowledge. Read the written material, practice using the worksheets and activities, and (above all) apply it on the job so that your training will transfer from this job aid to on-the-job performance improvement. For additional input, be sure to ask mentors or knowledgeable co-workers for one-on-one coaching.

SECTION 1 GETTING STARTED

SECTION 2 DEFINING THE ROLES

♦ The Role of the Manager
— Definition of the Role
— Importance of the Role
— The Relationship Between This and Other Roles
— The Place of the Manager in the Human Performance Improvement Process
— Competencies Associated With the Role of Manager
— Outputs Associated With the Role of Manager
— Who Performs the Role of Manager?
— When Do They Perform This Role?
— What Projects Do Managers of WLP Carry Out?

♦ The Role of the Change Leader
— Definition of the Role
— Importance of the Role
— The Relationship Between This and Other Roles
— The Place of the Change Leader in the Human Performance Improvement Process
— Competencies Associated With the Role of Change Leader
— Outputs Associated With the Role of Change Leader
— Who Performs the Role of Change Leader?
— When Do They Perform This Role?
— What Projects Do Change Leaders Carry Out?

SECTION 3 ENACTING THE ROLE OF MANAGER

SECTION 4 ENACTING THE ROLE OF CHANGE LEADER

SECTION 5 TOOLS FOR CONDUCTING MANAGEMENT AND CHANGE LEADERSHIP

SECTION 6   AFTERWORD

SECTION 7   BIBLIOGRAPHY

This section defines the roles of manager and change leader. This section also explains the importance of each role, describes how each role is related to other roles, shows the placement of each role in the human performance improvement (HPI) process, lists the competencies and outputs of each role, and reviews who performs each role, when those roles are carried out, and what projects are carried out by each role.

The Role of the Manager

Definition of the Role

The WLP practitioner's role as manager is to do the following: plan, organize, schedule, and lead the work of individuals and groups to attain desired results; facilitate the strategic plan; ensure that workplace learning and performance is aligned with organizational needs and plans; and ensure the accomplishment of the administrative requirements of the function. The manager sets the stage for the success of the WLP effort or function in an organization, runs interference to knock down barriers that may impede WLP staff performance, and generally sets the tone for a work environment that encourages people to achieve results to the peak of their abilities. It is often the case, too, that managers must familiarize themselves with the details of the work performed by their staff members as well as the organization for which they are working and set an example worthy of emulation.

Importance of the Role

Managers of WLP are responsible for creating the infrastructure (work environment) within which WLP practitioners perform. They have an important say in creating a vision for WLP in the organization, leveraging the WLP function to help meet important business needs, empowering staff members, supplying the resources that are essential to achieving results, and positioning the WLP function so that it partners with (and even leads) management in achieving quantum-leap and incremental breakthrough results with people.

Without the resources supplied by the manager and without an ability to manage up the organization's chain of command, no WLP function or department can be successful. On the one hand, the manager bears much responsibility for setting policy;

securing the people, data, and things necessary to achieve results; streamlining processes; and selecting, developing, rewarding, and recognizing staff. Without these activities, the WLP function or department could not last long as an effective department, function, or effort. On the other hand, a decision by others to outsource all or part of the WLP effort is usually evidence of failure in these activities.

It is worth noting that many managers with WLP responsibilities may be called upon to establish a corporate university. Jeanne Meister (1998) has outlined 10 key steps to creating a corporate university:

1. form a governing body
2. craft a vision
3. recommend the funding strategy
4. determine the scope
5. identify the stakeholders and their needs
6. develop products and services
7. select learning partners
8. draft a technology strategy
9. devise a measurement system
10. communicate the vision, products, and program.

These steps are also useful for managers of WLP departments to keep in mind, since the model is a general one with broad applicability to managing a WLP department or function as well as to setting up a corporate university.

The Relationship Between This and Other Roles

The manager ensures that others in an organization are aware of the purpose and mission of the WLP function, what activities it undertakes to realize that purpose and mission, and what results are yielded from those efforts.

The manager role guides and oversees all other WLP roles. First, and more specifically, the manager helps those WLP practitioners enacting the analyst role to select business problems or opportunities worthy of troubleshooting. Second, the manager of WLP makes suggestions to those enacting the intervention selector role about appropriate learning and performance interventions to choose, given the corporate culture, stakeholder values and preferences, resources available, and the organization's political issues. Third, the manager of WLP gives advice to those enacting the intervention designer and developer role about how to plan performance improvement interventions. Fourth, the manager of WLP coaches those enacting the intervention implementor role to ensure that delivery methods and implementation approaches match up to stakeholder needs, expectations, and business requirements. Fifth, the manager of WLP answers objections and concerns raised by stakeholders during intervention implementation and thereby provides assistance to the change leader role. Sixth and finally, the manager of WLP insists on the need for establishing a tracking and monitoring system and thereby sets the stage for those WLP practitioners who enact the evaluator role.

In large organizations, the roles may be distinctive, with some individuals assigned specific responsibilities. In small organizations, however, the manager of WLP may have to do it all—and be a one-person powerhouse responsible for enacting all the roles (Taylor, 1998).

The Place of the Manager in the Human Performance Improvement Process

The manager is responsible for oversight of all steps in the HPI process model, the guiding model for WLP, as shown in figure 2.1. The manager establishes and carries out the strategy for the WLP department, function, or effort with others in the organization.

Competencies Associated With the Role of Manager

Descriptions of the competencies associated with the manager role can be found in Rothwell, Sanders, and Soper (1999) and are shown in table 2.1. These competencies represent a daunting skill set. To summarize what they mean in practice, managers should be capable of exercising oversight over WLP efforts.

First, managers of WLP must clarify complex issues by breaking them down into meaningful components and synthesizing related items (*analytical thinking*), and they must perform front-end analysis by comparing actual and ideal performance levels in the workplace to identify opportunities and strategies for performance improvement (*performance gap analysis*).

Second, managers of WLP must identify the skills, knowledge, and attitudes required to perform work (*competency identification*); develop and implement systems for creating, managing, and distributing knowledge (*knowledge management*); measure knowledge capital and determine its value to the organization (*knowledge capital*); and recognize the implications, outcomes, and consequences of performance interventions to distinguish between activities and results (*performance theory*).

Third, WLP managers must possess what might be called strategic abilities, and these include leading, influencing, and coaching others to help them achieve desired results (*leadership*); seeing the possibilities of

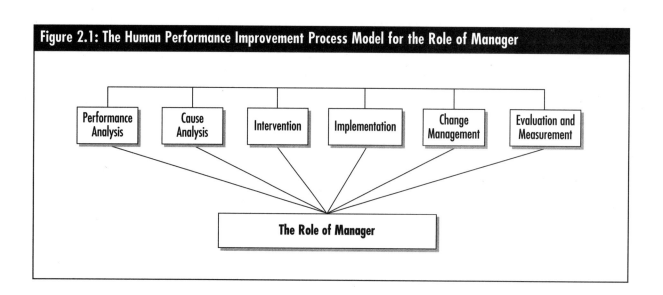

Figure 2.1: The Human Performance Improvement Process Model for the Role of Manager

Performance Analysis | Cause Analysis | Intervention | Implementation | Change Management | Evaluation and Measurement

The Role of Manager

Table 2.1: Competencies Associated with the Manager's Role

♦ *Ability to see the big picture:* Identifying trends and patterns that are outside the normal paradigm of the organization.

♦ *Analtyical thinking:* Clarifying complex issues by breaking them down into meaningful components and synthesizing related items.

♦ *Business knowledge:* Demonstrating awareness of business functions and how business decisions affect financial and nonfinancial work results.

♦ *Buy-in advocacy:* Building ownership and support for workplace initiatives.

♦ *Career development theory and application:* Understanding the theories, techniques, and appropriate applications of career development interventions used for performance improvement.

♦ *Communication:* Applying effective verbal, nonverbal, and written communication methods to achieve desired results.

♦ *Communication networks:* Understanding the various methods through which communication is achieved.

♦ *Competency identification:* Identifying the skills, knowledge, and attitudes required to perform work.

♦ *Computer-mediated communication:* Understanding the implication of current and evolving computer-based electronic communication.

♦ *Consulting:* Understanding the results that stakeholders desire from a process and providing insight into how they can best use their resources to achieve goals.

♦ *Coping skills:* Dealing with ambiguity and stress resulting from conflicting information and goals; helping others deal with ambiguity and stress.

♦ *Cost-benefit analysis:* Accurately assessing the relative value of performance improvement interventions.

♦ *Diversity awareness:* Assessing the impact and appropriateness of interventions on individuals, groups, and organizations.

♦ *Ethics modeling:* Modeling exemplary ethical behavior and understanding the implications of this responsibility.

♦ *Evaluation of results against organizational goals:* Assessing how well workplace performance, learning strategies, and results match organizational goals and strategic intent.

♦ *Facilitation:* Helping others to discover new insights.

♦ *Feedback:* Providing performance information to the appropriate people.

♦ *Group dynamics:* Assessing how groups of people function and evolve as they seek to meet the needs of their members and of the organization.

♦ *Identification of critical business issues:* Determining key business issues and forces for change and applying that knowledge to performance improvement strategies.

♦ *Industry awareness:* Understanding the current and future climate of the organization's industry and formulating strategies that respond to that climate.

♦ *Interpersonal relationship building:* Effectively interacting with others in order to produce meaningful outcomes.

♦ *Knowledge capital:* Measuring knowledge capital and determining its value to the organization.

♦ *Knowledge management:* Developing and implementing systems for creating, managing, and distributing knowledge.

(continued on next page)

Table 2.1: Competencies Associated with the Manager's Role *(continued)*

- *Leadership*: Leading, influencing, and coaching others to help them achieve desired results.

- *Negotiating and contracting*: Organizing, preparing, monitoring, and evaluating work performed by vendors and consultants.

- *Organization development theory and application*: Understanding the theories, techniques, and appropriate applications of organization development interventions as they are used for performance improvement.

- *Outsourcing management*: Ability to identify and select specialized resources outside of the organization; identifying, selecting, and managing technical specifications for these specialized resources.

- *Performance gap analysis*: Performing front-end analysis by comparing actual and ideal performance levels in the workplace; identifying opportunities and strategies for performance improvement.

- *Performance theory*: Recognizing the implications, outcomes, and consequences of performance interventions to distinguish between activities and results.

- *Process consultation*: Using a monitoring and feedback method to continually improve the productivity of work groups.

- *Project management*: Planning, organizing, and monitoring work.

- *Quality implications*: Identifying the relationships and implications among quality programs and performance.

- *Reward system theory and application*: Understanding the theories, techniques, and appropriate applications of reward system interventions used for performance improvement.

- *Social awareness*: Seeing organizations as dynamic political, economic, and social systems.

- *Staff selection theory and application*: Understanding the theories, techniques, and appropriate applications of staff selection interventions used for performance improvement.

- *Standards identification*: Determining what constitutes success for individuals, organizations, and processes.

- *Systems thinking*: Recognizing the interrelationship among events by determining the driving forces that connect seemingly isolated incidents within the organization; taking a holistic view of performance problems in order to find root causes.

- *Technological literacy*: Understanding and appropriately applying existing, new, or emerging technology.

- *Visioning*: Seeing the possibilities of what can be and inspiring a shared sense of purpose within the organization.

- *Work environment analysis*: Examining the work environment for issues or characteristics that affect human performance; understanding characteristics of a high performance workplace.

Source: Rothwell, W., Sanders, E., and Soper, J. (1999). *ASTD Models for Workplace Learning and Performance: Roles, Competencies, and Outputs.* Alexandria, VA: ASTD, pp. 53–56. Used by permission.

what can be and inspiring a shared sense of purpose within the organization (*visioning*); determining key business issues and forces for change and applying that knowledge to performance improvement strategies (*identification of critical business issues*); understanding the current and future climate of the organization's industry and formulating strategies that respond to that climate (*industry awareness*); determining what constitutes success for individuals, organizations, and processes (*standards identification*); recognizing the interrelationship among events by determining the driving forces that connect seemingly isolated incidents within the organization; taking a holistic view of performance problems in order to find root causes (*systems thinking*); examining the work environment for issues or characteristics that affect human performance; understanding characteristics of a high performance workplace (*work environment analysis*); identifying trends and patterns that are outside the normal paradigm of the organization (*ability to see the big picture*); demonstrating awareness of business functions and how business decisions affect financial and nonfinancial work results (*business knowledge*); and assessing how well workplace performance, learning strategies, and results match organizational goals and strategic intent (*evaluation of results against organizational goals*).

Fourth, managers of WLP should be versed in a range of theories and applications, including understanding the theories, techniques, and appropriate applications of career development interventions used for performance improvement (*career development theory and application*); understanding the theories, techniques, and appropriate applications of organization development interventions as they are used for performance improvement (*organization development theory and application*); understanding the theories, techniques, and appropriate applications of reward system interventions used for performance improvement (*reward system theory and application*); and understanding the theories, techniques, and appropriate applications of staff selection interventions used for performance improvement (*staff selection theory and application*).

Fifth, managers of WLP must be skilled in dealing with people by using a monitoring and feedback method to continually improve the productivity of work groups (*process consultation*); seeing organizations as dynamic political, economic, and social systems (*social awareness*); applying effective verbal, nonverbal, and written communication methods to achieve desired results (*communication*); understanding the various methods through which communication is achieved (*communication networks*); understanding the results that stakeholders desire from a process and providing insight into how they can best use their resources to achieve goals (*consulting*); dealing with ambiguity and stress resulting from conflicting information and goals; helping others deal with ambiguity and stress (*coping skills*); effectively interacting with others in order to produce meaningful outcomes (*interpersonal relationship building*); building ownership and support for workplace initiatives (*buy-in advocacy*); assessing the impact and appropriateness of interventions on individuals, groups, and organizations (*diversity awareness*); helping others to discover new insights (*facilitation*); providing performance information to the appropriate people (*feedback*); and assessing how groups of people function and evolve as they seek to meet the needs of their members and of the organization (*group dynamics*).

Finally, managers of WLP share many competencies with many other managers, including accurately assessing the relative value of performance improvement interventions (*cost-benefit analysis*); organizing, preparing, monitoring, and evaluating work performed by vendors and consultants (*negotiating and contracting*); identifying and selecting specialized resources outside of the organization; identifying, selecting, and managing technical specifications for these specialized resources (*outsourcing management*); planning, organizing, and monitoring work (*project management*); identifying the relationships and implications among quality programs and performance (*quality implications*); modeling exemplary ethical behavior and understanding the implications of this responsibility (*ethics modeling*); understanding the implication of current and evolving computer-based electronic communication (*computer-mediated communication*); and understanding and appropriately applying existing, new, or emerging technology (*technological literacy*).

Outputs Associated With the Role of Manager

Output is the term used to refer to the results of the management processes. (For examples of outputs linked to this role, see table 2.2.) However, the specific work outputs necessary in the role depend upon the unique requirements of key stakeholders, an organization's unique corporate culture, and work expectations. Take a moment to consider the corporate culture and work expectations of your own organization by completing the worksheet in figure 2.2. Use the results of this worksheet to help you clarify the expectations of your customers and stakeholders for how you should enact the role of WLP manager.

Who Performs the Role of Manager?

The role of manager—like that of other WLP roles—may be played by WLP practitioners who oversee a WLP department, function, or effort. The

Table 2.2: Sample Outputs Associated with the Manager's Role

- ◆ WLP plans for the organization or unit
- ◆ Strategies that align WLP efforts with organizational and individual needs
- ◆ Work plans for WLP efforts
- ◆ Plans to secure the human talent to carry out WLP efforts
- ◆ Objectives that support desired business results

Source: Rothwell, W., Sanders, E., and Soper, J. (1999). *ASTD Models for Workplace Learning and Performance: Roles, Competencies, and Outputs.* Alexandria, VA: ASTD, p. 61. Used by permission.

Figure 2.2: Worksheet to Organize Your Thinking on the Work Expectations of Your Organization for the Manager's Role

Directions: Use this worksheet to organize your thinking about the work expectations your organization has for you in your role as manager of WLP. Remember that the role of manager "plans, organizes, schedules, monitors, and leads the work of individuals and groups to attain desired results; facilitates the strategic plan; ensures that WLP is aligned with organizational needs and plans; and ensures accomplishment of the administrative requirements of the function" (Rothwell, Sanders, and Soper, 1999, p. 43). However, the outputs and quality requirements of the manager role may vary from one corporate culture to another. For each competency listed in column 1, describe in column 2 what results—outputs—you believe your organization expects. (You may need to discuss this issue with key decision makers and stakeholders in your organization.) Then, in column 3, describe what behaviors and quality requirements, or both, would demonstrate success with that competency. In short, what results would you have to obtain to be considered successful by your customers and stakeholders? While there are no "right" or "wrong" answers to these questions in any absolute sense, they are important for building the appropriate expectations among your customers and stakeholders. Take the time to discuss these issues.

	Column 1 Competency	Column 2 What do you believe are the organization's expectations for results—the outputs—for your functioning in the manager role in your organization?	Column 3 What behavior and quality requirements would demonstrate success with this competency in this organization? In short, what results would you have to obtain to be considered successful by your customers and stakeholders?
1	*Ability to see the big picture:* Identifying trends and patterns that are outside the normal paradigm of the organization.		
2	*Analytical thinking:* Clarifying complex issues by breaking them down into meaningful components and synthesizing related items.		

3	*Business knowledge:* Demonstrating awareness of business functions and how business decisions affect financial and nonfinancial work results.		
4	*Buy-in advocacy:* Building ownership and support for workplace initiatives.		
5	*Career development theory and application:* Understanding the theories, techniques, and appropriate applications of career development interventions used for performance improvement.		
6	*Communication:* Applying effective verbal, nonverbal, and written communication methods to achieve desired results.		
7	*Communication networks:* Understanding the various methods through which communication is achieved.		
8	*Competency identification:* Identifying the skills, knowledge, and attitudes required to perform work.		
9	*Computer-mediated communication:* Understanding the implication of current and evolving computer-based electronic communication.		
10	*Consulting:* Understanding the results that stakeholders desire from a process and providing insight into how they can best use their resources to achieve goals.		

(continued on next page)

Figure 2.2: Worksheet to Organize Your Thinking on the Work Expectations of Your Organization for the Manager's Role *(continued)*

Column 1 Competency	Column 2 What do you believe are the organization's expectations for results—the outputs—for your functioning in the manager role in your organization?	Column 3 What behavior and quality requirements would demonstrate success with this competency in this organization? In short, what results would you have to obtain to be considered successful by your customers and stakeholders?
11 *Coping skills:* Dealing with ambiguity and stress resulting from conflicting information and goals; helping others deal with ambiguity and stress.		
12 *Cost-benefit analysis:* Accurately assessing the relative value of performance improvement interventions.		
13 *Diversity awareness:* Assessing the impact and appropriateness of interventions on individuals, groups, and organizations.		
14 *Ethics modeling:* Modeling exemplary ethical behavior and understanding the implications of this responsibility.		
15 *Evaluation of results against organizational goals:* Assessing how well workplace performance, learning strategies, and results match organizational goals and strategic intent.		
16 *Facilitation:* Helping others to discover new insights.		
17 *Feedback:* Providing performance information to the appropriate people.		

18	*Group dynamics:* Assessing how groups of people function and evolve as they seek to meet the needs of their members and of the organization.		
19	*Identification of critical business issues:* Determining key business issues and forces for change and applying that knowledge to performance improvement strategies.		
20	*Industry awareness:* Understanding the current and future climate of the organization's industry and formulating strategies that respond to that climate.		
21	*Interpersonal relationship building:* Effectively interacting with others in order to produce meaningful outcomes.		
22	*Knowledge capital:* Measuring knowledge capital and determining its value to the organization.		
23	*Knowledge management:* Developing and implementing systems for creating, managing, and distributing knowledge.		
24	*Leadership:* Leading, influencing, and coaching others to help them achieve desired results.		
25	*Negotiating and contracting:* Organizing, preparing, monitoring, and evaluating work performed by vendors and consultants.		

(continued on next page)

Figure 2.2: Worksheet to Organize Your Thinking on the Work Expectations of Your Organization for the Manager's Role (continued)

	Column 1 Competency	Column 2 What do you believe are the organization's expectations for results—the outputs—for your functioning in the manager role in your organization?	Column 3 What behavior and quality requirements would demonstrate success with this competency in this organization? In short, what results would you have to obtain to be considered successful by your customers and stakeholders?
26	*Organization development theory and application:* Understanding the theories, techniques, and appropriate applications of organization development interventions as they are used for performance improvement.		
27	*Outsourcing management:* Ability to identify and select specialized resources outside of the organization; identifying, selecting, and managing technical specifications for these specialized resources.		
28	*Performance gap analysis:* Performing front-end analysis by comparing actual and ideal performance levels in the workplace; identifying opportunities and strategies for performance improvement.		
29	*Performance theory:* Recognizing the implications, outcomes, and consequences of performance interventions to distinguish between activities and results.		
30	*Process consultation:* Using a monitoring and feedback method to continually improve the productivity of work groups.		

31	*Project management:* Planning, organizing, and monitoring work.		
32	*Quality implications:* Identifying the relationships and implications among quality programs and performance.		
33	*Reward system theory and application:* Understanding the theories, techniques, and appropriate applications of reward system interventions used for performance improvement.		
34	*Social awareness:* Seeing organizations as dynamic political, economic, and social systems.		
35	*Staff selection theory and application:* Understanding the theories, techniques, and appropriate applications of staff selection interventions used for performance improvement.		
36	*Standards identification:* Determining what constitutes success for individuals, organizations, and processes.		
37	*Systems thinking:* Recognizing the interrelationship among events by determining the driving forces that connect seemingly isolated incidents within the organization; taking a holistic view of performance problems in order to find root causes.		
38	*Technological literacy:* Understanding and appropriately applying existing, new, or emerging technology.		

(continued on next page)

Figure 2.2: Worksheet to Organize Your Thinking on the Work Expectations of Your Organization for the Manager's Role (continued)

	Column 1 Competency	Column 2 What do you believe are the organization's expectations for results—the outputs—for your functioning in the manager role in your organization?	Column 3 What behavior and quality requirements would demonstrate success with this competency in this organization? In short, what results would you have to obtain to be considered successful by your customers and stakeholders?
39	*Visioning:* Seeing the possibilities of what can be and inspiring a shared sense of purpose within the organization.		
40	*Work environment analysis:* Examining the work environment for issues or characteristics that affect human performance; understanding characteristics of a high performance workplace.		

manager role may also be carried out by those serving as external or internal consultants, outsourcing agents or vendors, line managers, employees, or any or all of the above. Anyone who oversees other people bears some responsibility for managing WLP. Anyone who has broad scope responsibilities for oversight of one or more WLP efforts or projects must essentially enact the role of manager of WLP.

When Do They Perform This Role?

The management of WLP is carried out during supervision of people. It is integral to any management role. However, some individuals may be assigned full-time responsibility for oversight of a WLP department, and they must bear full-time responsibility for the role of WLP manager.

What Projects Do Managers of WLP Carry Out?

Managers of WLP are responsible for setting the agenda and exerting leadership for the organization's WLP efforts.

While they do not have sole responsibility, they do frame the issues and provide structure and

organization for planning WLP efforts, whether learning interventions or nonlearning interventions. Their role is to facilitate decision making with all managers and workers of an organization and, when assigned, with such other stakeholder groups as customers, suppliers, distributors, and other relevant groups.

The Role of the Change Leader

Definition of the Role

The WLP practitioner's role as change leader is to inspire the workforce to embrace the interventions implemented, create a direction for the effort, and ensure that interventions are continuously monitored and directed in ways that are consistent with stakeholders' desired results. This role may, perhaps, be summarized in two words—*follow through*. By following through, the change leader ensures that interventions are accepted and benefit from stakeholder ownership. The role of change leader is often associated with that of the organization development (OD) practitioner (Rothwell,

Sullivan, and McLean, 1995) and with that of the HR champion (Ulrich, 1997).

Change leaders guide others through the seven quantum leap skills that Shelton (1999) identified as being essential for workplace change:

♦ seeing

♦ thinking

♦ feeling

♦ knowing

♦ acting

♦ trusting

♦ being.

To ensure effective change leadership, the organization must establish a reporting structure conducive to the change, establish incentives and rewards that are related to desired results (Hawk, 1995), ensure that organizational policies are made consistent with the desired change results, and encourage through positive influence what people should do to achieve desired results (Rothwell and Kazanas, 1994a).

It is a mistake to assume that WLP practitioners are the only ones with a role to play in change leadership. Middle managers play an essential role. Unfortunately, though, one research study found that only 10 percent of middle managers function effectively as change leaders (Sherman, 1995). But middle managers, more than top managers, play a critical role in change leadership, and their support is really a "make or break issue" for the success of a change effort or a performance improvement intervention (Katzenbach and others, 1995; Katzenbach, 1996).

Change leaders do not act independently of other roles. Relying on the results of the analyst's role, change leaders ensure that interventions are carried out to solve performance problems. Change leaders venture beyond the role of intervention implementor, the role with which they are often most closely associated, because change leaders garner support and buy-in through involving, empowering, and energizing the workforce to participate fully in an intervention. They exert positive influence by capturing the support and building infectious enthusiasm among others, a particularly challenging task when dealing with a skeptical or even cynical workforce. As Kiser (1998) has pointed out, effective change leaders are masterful facilitators who successfully make and keep contact with all those involved in a change effort. They serve an important role by clarifying desired intervention or change objectives, contracting with stakeholders and change participants for achieving results, designing the intervention on a tactical level, facilitating ongoing change, and evaluating tactical-level (daily) results.

If the analyst's role is akin to that of the medical doctor who serves as diagnostician, and the intervention selector's role is akin to that of the medical doctor who prescribes medicine, then the change leader's role is akin to that of the medical doctor whose empathetic bedside manner encourages patients to take care of themselves and comply with the therapeutic routine leading to better health. Doctors who make the rounds in a hospital to check on their patients are enacting their own role of change leaders. Following through on a detailed level—a role more often played in medicine by nurses rather than by doctors—is exactly akin to what change leaders in WLP must do to track the progress of a performance improvement intervention.

Change leadership is thus the process of inspiring and encouraging people during an intervention. (The term *intervention* is typically used instead of *solution* to imply more than a quick fix.) Change leadership is not just a matter of ensuring that everyone gets along; rather, it involves helping employees to understand their organizations, their organizations' customers, and the business environment ("Bringing Sears Into the New World," 1997).

Change leaders can use many approaches to encourage change. While they can try to persuade or sell the benefits of an intervention, they are more often involved in harnessing group creativity and group action to solve specific group problems that occur during the implementation of an intervention. Like intervention implementors, they can rely on such methods as the action research model of organization development, which gathers information about problems from those involved in the change effort and then feeds back that information to make a compelling case for change and to create excitement about the change. Alternatively, they may build on strengths by using appreciative inquiry to pinpoint what is going right and spark creative thinking about ways to encourage, enhance, and further develop what is going right.

Importance of the Role

No intervention can be successful unless someone follows through to ensure that ambitious plans turn into concrete actions. Most interventions last a long time. In fact, interventions that call for change in an entire organization may take years to install effectively, since changes in corporate culture do not happen overnight. Always remember that people become disappointed if they do not see some quick successes, but rarely does dramatic change in a large organization occur unless someone takes charge as a change leader and champions the effort.

The change leader's role is important because most decision makers want results and not the glitzy but specious appearance of action taken to address problems (which is called window dressing) or a quickly chosen solution that eventually causes more problems than it solves (which is called shooting-from-the-hip decision making).

The Relationship Between This and Other Roles

The change leader's role depends on the work results of all other roles. The change leader thus builds on the work of the manager, analyst, intervention selector, intervention designer and developer, intervention implementor, and evaluator. The key to success as a change leader is to excite enthusiasm for the change embodied in an intervention and to keep up the change impetus despite conflicting priorities or slippage (that is, the return to a prechange state).

The Place of the Change Leader in the Human Performance Improvement Process

The change leader is positioned near the end of the HPI process model, the guiding model for workplace learning and performance, as shown in figure 2.3. Note that change leadership should only occur after all the steps in the HRI process model have been followed.

Competencies Associated With the Role of Change Leader

Descriptions of the research-based competencies associated with the change leader's role can be found in Rothwell, Sanders, and Soper (1999) and are shown in table 2.3. The competencies listed in the table can be summarized in a sentence: Change leaders should be able to excite enthusiasm about an intervention among all the stakeholders participating in it and affected by it. Effective change leaders, according to research conducted by Hooper (1999), successfully do the following: communicate the reasons for change, release everyone to be involved in contributing to the change, provide a good personal example, and keep the stress associated with a change effort manageable. When carried out on a daily basis, those activities are, of course, far more challenging than they sound.

Outputs Associated With the Role of Change Leader

Output is the term used to refer to the results of change leadership processes. (For examples of the

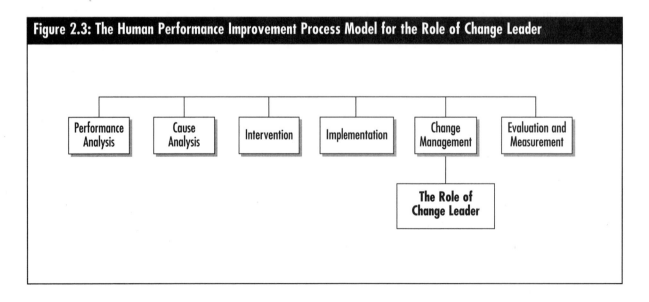

Figure 2.3: The Human Performance Improvement Process Model for the Role of Change Leader

| Performance Analysis | Cause Analysis | Intervention | Implementation | Change Management | Evaluation and Measurement |

The Role of Change Leader

Table 2.3: Competencies Associated with the Change Leader's Role

- *Ability to see the big picture:* Identifying trends and patterns that are outside the normal paradigm of the organization.

- *Adult learning:* Understanding how adults learn and how they use knowledge, skills, and attitudes.

- *Analytical thinking:* Clarifying complex issues by breaking them down into meaningful components and synthesizing related items.

- *Analyzing performance data:* Interpreting performance data and determining the effect of interventions on customers, suppliers, and employees.

- *Business knowledge:* Demonstrating awareness of business functions and how business decisions affect financial and nonfinancial work results.

- *Buy-in advocacy:* Building ownership and support for workplace initiatives.

- *Career development theory and application:* Understanding the theories, techniques, and appropriate applications of career development interventions used for performance improvement.

- *Communication:* Applying effective verbal, nonverbal, and written communication methods to achieve desired results.

- *Communication networks:* Understanding the various methods through which communication is achieved.

- *Computer-mediated communication:* Understanding the implication of current and evolving computer-based electronic communication.

- *Consulting:* Understanding the results that stakeholders desire from a process and providing insight into how they can best use their resources to achieve goals.

- *Coping skills:* Dealing with ambiguity and stress resulting from conflicting information and goals; helping others deal with ambiguity and stress.

- *Diversity awareness:* Assessing the impact and appropriateness of interventions on individuals, groups, and organizations.

- *Ethics modeling:* Modeling exemplary ethical behavior and understanding the implications of this responsibility.

- *Evaluation of results against organizational goals:* Assessing how well workplace performance, learning strategies, and results match organizational goals and strategic intent.

- *Facilitation:* Helping others to discover new insights.

- *Feedback:* Providing performance information to the appropriate people.

- *Group dynamics:* Assessing how groups of people function and evolve as they seek to meet the needs of their members and of the organization.

- *Identification of critical business issues:* Determining key business issues and forces for change and applying that knowledge to performance improvement strategies.

- *Industry awareness:* Understanding the current and future climate of the organization's industry and formulating strategies that respond to that climate.

- *Interpersonal relationship building:* Effectively interacting with others in order to produce meaningful outcomes.

- *Intervention monitoring:* Tracking and coordinating interventions to ensure consistency in implementation and alignment with organizational strategies.

- *Knowledge capital:* Measuring knowledge capital and determining its value to the organization.

(continued on next page)

Table 2.3: Competencies Associated with the Change Leader's Role *(continued)*

- *Knowledge management:* Developing and implementing systems for creating, managing, and distributing knowledge.
- *Leadership:* Leading, influencing, and coaching others to help them achieve desired results.
- *Model building:* Conceptualizing and developing theoretical and practical frameworks that describe complex ideas.
- *Organization development theory and application:* Understanding the theories, techniques, and appropriate applications of organization development interventions as they are used for performance improvement.
- *Outsourcing management:* Ability to identify and select specialized resources outside of the organization; identifying, selecting, and managing technical specifications for these specialized resources.
- *Performance theory:* Recognizing the implications, outcomes, and consequences of performance interventions to distinguish between activities and results.
- *Process consultation:* Using a monitoring and feedback method to continually improve the productivity of work groups.
- *Project management:* Planning, organizing, and monitoring work.
- *Quality implications:* Identifying the relationships and implications among quality programs and performance.
- *Reward system theory and application:* Understanding the theories, techniques, and appropriate applications of reward system interventions used for performance improvement.
- *Social awareness:* Seeing organizations as dynamic political, economic, and social systems.
- *Staff selection theory and application:* Understanding the theories, techniques, and appropriate applications of staff selection interventions used for performance improvement.
- *Standards identification:* Determining what constitutes success for individuals, organizations, and processes.
- *Systems thinking:* Recognizing the interrelationship among events by determining the driving forces that connect seemingly isolated incidents within the organization; taking a holistic view of performance problems in order to find root causes.
- *Technological literacy:* Understanding and appropriately applying existing, new, or emerging technology.
- *Training theory and application:* Understanding the theories, techniques, and appropriate applications of training interventions for performance improvement.
- *Visioning:* Seeing the possibilities of what can be and inspiring a shared sense of purpose within the organization.
- *Work environment analysis:* Examining the work environment for issues or characteristics that affect human performance; understanding characteristics of a high-performance workplace.
- *Workplace performance, learning strategies, and intervention evaluation:* Continually evaluating and improving interventions before and during implementation..

Source: Rothwell, W., Sanders, E., and Soper, J. (1999). *ASTD Models for Workplace Learning and Performance: Roles, Competencies, and Outputs.* Alexandria, VA: ASTD, pp. 53–56. Used by permission.

outputs of the change leader role, see table 2.4.) However, the particular work outputs necessary in the change leader's role depend upon the unique requirements of key stakeholders, an organization's corporate culture, and work expectations. Take a moment to consider the corporate culture and work expectations of your own organization by completing the worksheet in figure 2.4.

Who Performs the Role of Change Leader?

The role of change leader may be played by one or more of the following: WLP practitioners serving as external or internal consultants, line managers, or employees. There are distinctive advantages and disadvantages for choosing each of these groups to play the change leader role.

External consultants often possess expertise and command credibility in the subject in question and experience in selecting appropriate interventions. These are distinct advantages to using them as change leaders. Evidence of expertise, such as an academic degree, a successful track record, or publications on the subject, may make it easier for external consultants to gain access to key stakeholders. They may also have license to ask questions or recommend approaches that might not otherwise be acceptable for an internal consultant in the corporate culture.

But external consultants may also possess disadvantages as change leaders. They are not as familiar with an organization's corporate culture, power structure, or work processes as internal consultants, line managers, or employees are. Nor do they know the personalities or value systems of the organization's key decision makers. External consultants must find ways to familiarize themselves with such

matters quickly and effectively. They are also expensive to use for daily follow-up and follow-through on interventions.

Internal consultants as change leaders also offer a number of advantages. They are usually more familiar than external consultants with the particular industry or business, the organization's corporate culture, and work processes. Additionally, internal consultants can afford the time and effort to exert day-to-day change leadership in a way that may not be possible for external consultants who have other clients and other demands on their time.

But internal consultants present disadvantages as change leaders, just as external consultants do. They may not be able to gain access to key decision makers, and they may not be considered as credible as external consultants. Further, internal consultants' objectivity in cheering on change efforts is often questionable, especially if they are trying to "sell" something that they can do. Stakeholders may even accuse them on occasion of manipulating daily results of an intervention so that they can sell additional consulting services, a "crime" that external consultants are likewise accused of doing.

Of course, line managers and employees are most familiar with the daily routine of the work and the influence of a performance improvement intervention on it. But that familiarity has its disadvantage. While they may know what is happening on a very detailed level, they may not be able to inspire others to be enthusiastic about necessary changes or even to see the need for them. Of course, line managers and employees alike can be trained in the competencies of the change leader's role, just as they can be trained in the competencies of other WLP roles.

Table 2.4: Sample Outputs Associated with the Change Leader's Role

♦ Revised implementation plans that reflect changes in the original intervention strategy
♦ Periodic reports to key stakeholders of interventions about their progress
♦ Written illustrations of successful implementation cases

Source: Rothwell, W., Sanders, E., and Soper, J. (1999). *ASTD Models for Workplace Learning and Performance: Roles, Competencies, and Outputs.* Alexandria, VA: ASTD, p. 61. Used by permission.

Figure 2.4: Worksheet to Organize Your Thinking on the Work Expectations of Your Organization for the Change Leader's Role

Directions: Use this worksheet to organize your thinking about the work expectations your organization has for you in your role as change leader. Remember that the role of the change leader "inspires the workforce to embrace the change, creates a direction for the change effort, helps the organization's workforce to adapt to the change, and ensures that interventions are continuously monitored and guided in ways consistent with stakeholders' desired results" (Rothwell, Sanders, and Soper, 1999, p. 43). However, the outputs and quality requirements of the change leader role may vary from one corporate culture to another. For each competency listed in column 1, describe in column 2 what results—outputs—you believe your organization expects. (You may need to discuss this issue with your organization's key decision makers and stakeholders.) Then, in column 3, describe what behaviors and quality requirements would demonstrate success with that competency. In short, what results would you have to obtain to be considered successful by your customers and stakeholders? While there are no "right" or "wrong" answers to these questions in any absolute sense, they are important for building the appropriate expectations among your customers and stakeholders. Take the time to discuss these issues.

	Column 1 Competency	Column 2 What do you believe are the organization's expectations for results—the outputs—for your functioning in the change leader role in your organization?	Column 3 What behavior and quality requirements would demonstrate success with this competency in this organization? In short, what results would you have to obtain to be considered successful by your customers and stakeholders?
1	*Ability to see the big picture:* Identifying trends and patterns that are outside the normal paradigm of the organization.		
2	*Adult learning:* Understanding how adults learn and how they use knowledge, skills, and attitudes.		
3	*Analytical thinking:* Clarifying complex issues by breaking them down into meaningful components and synthesizing related items.		
4	*Analyzing performance data:* Interpreting performance data and determining the effect of interventions on customers, suppliers, and employees.		

5	*Business knowledge:* Demonstrating awareness of business functions and how business decisions affect financial and nonfinancial work results.		
6	*Buy-in advocacy:* Building ownership and support for workplace initiatives.		
7	*Career development theory and application:* Understanding the theories, techniques, and appropriate applications of career development interventions used for performance improvement.		
8	*Communication:* Applying effective verbal, nonverbal, and written communication methods to achieve desired results.		
9	*Communication networks:* Understanding the various methods through which communication is achieved.		
10	*Computer-mediated communication:* Understanding the implication of current and evolving computer-based electronic communication.		
11	*Consulting:* Understanding the results that stakeholders desire from a process and providing insight into how they can best use their resources to achieve goals.		
12	*Coping skills:* Dealing with ambiguity and stress resulting from conflicting information and goals; helping others deal with ambiguity and stress.		

(continued on next page)

	Column 1 **Competency**	Column 2 **What do you believe are the organization's expectations for results—the outputs—for your functioning in the change leader role in your organization?**	Column 3 **What behavior and quality requirements would demonstrate success with this competency in this organization? In short, what results would you have to obtain to be considered successful by your customers and stakeholders?**
13	*Diversity awareness:* Assessing the impact and appropriateness of interventions on individuals, groups, and organizations.		
14	*Ethics modeling:* Modeling exemplary ethical behavior and understanding the implications of this responsibility.		
15	*Evaluation of results against organizational goals:* Assessing how well workplace performance, learning strategies, and results match organizational goals and strategic intent.		
16	*Facilitation:* Helping others to discover new insights.		
17	*Feedback:* Providing performance information to the appropriate people.		
18	*Group dynamics:* Assessing how groups of people function and evolve as they seek to meet the needs of their members and of the organization.		
19	*Identification of critical business issues:* Determining key business issues and forces for change and applying that knowledge to performance improvement strategies.		

20	*Industry awareness:* Understanding the current and future climate of the organization's industry and formulating strategies that respond to that climate.		
21	*Interpersonal relationship building:* Effectively interacting with others in order to produce meaningful outcomes.		
22	*Intervention monitoring:* Tracking and coordinating interventions to ensure consistency in implementation and alignment with organizational strategies.		
23	*Knowledge capital:* Measuring knowledge capital and determining its value to the organization.		
24	*Knowledge management:* Developing and implementing systems for creating, managing, and distributing knowledge.		
25	*Leadership:* Leading, influencing, and coaching others to help them achieve desired results.		
26	*Model building:* Conceptualizing and developing theoretical and practical frameworks that describe complex ideas.		
27	*Organization development theory and application:* Understanding the theories, techniques, and appropriate applications of organization development interventions as they are used for performance improvement.		

(continued on next page)

	Column 1 Competency	Column 2 What do you believe are the organization's expectations for results—the outputs—for your functioning in the change leader role in your organization?	Column 3 What behavior and quality requirements would demonstrate success with this competency in this organization? In short, what results would you have to obtain to be considered successful by your customers and stakeholders?
28	*Outsourcing management:* Ability to identify and select specialized resources outside of the organization; identifying, selecting, and managing technical specifications for these specialized resources.		
29	*Performance theory:* Recognizing the implications, outcomes, and consequences of performance interventions to distinguish between activities and results.		
30	*Process consultation:* Using a monitoring and feedback method to continually improve the productivity of work groups.		
31	*Project management:* Planning, organizing, and monitoring work.		
32	*Quality implications:* Identifying the relationships and implications among quality programs and performance.		
33	*Reward system theory and application:* Understanding the theories, techniques, and appropriate applications of reward system interventions used for performance improvement.		

34	*Social awareness:* Seeing organizations as dynamic political, economic, and social systems.		
35	*Staff selection theory and application:* Understanding the theories, techniques, and appropriate applications of staff selection interventions used for performance improvement.		
36	*Standards identification:* Determining what constitutes success for individuals, organizations, and processes.		
37	*Systems thinking:* Recognizing the interrelationship among events by determining the driving forces that connect seemingly isolated incidents within the organization; taking a holistic view of performance problems in order to find root causes.		
38	*Technological literacy:* Understanding and appropriately applying existing, new, or emerging technology.		
39	*Training theory and application:* Understanding the theories, techniques, and appropriate applications of training interventions for performance improvement.		
40	*Visioning:* Seeing the possibilities of what can be and inspiring a shared sense of purpose within the organization.		

(continued on next page)

Figure 2.4: Worksheet to Organize Your Thinking on the Work Expectations of Your Organization for the Change Leader's Role *(continued)*

	Column 1 Competency	Column 2 What do you believe are the organization's expectations for results—the outputs—for your functioning in the change leader role in your organization?	Column 3 What behavior and quality requirements would demonstrate success with this competency in this organization? In short, what results would you have to obtain to be considered successful by your customers and stakeholders?
41	*Work environment analysis:* Examining the work environment for issues or characteristics that affect human performance; understanding characteristics of a high-performance workplace.		
42	*Workplace performance, learning strategies, and intervention evaluation:* Continually evaluating and improving interventions before and during implementation.		

Often the most powerful approach for change leadership, as with other steps in the HPI process model, is to field a team of people to work on a detailed implementation and inspirational plan with others during an intervention. That team may include external consultants working along with internal ones; external consultants working with line managers or employees, or both; or internal consultants working with line managers or employees, or both.

When Do They Perform This Role?

As with other roles, the change leader's role can be undertaken when it is requested by others or is initiated by people acting on their own.

When Requested by Others. WLP practitioners are familiar with occasions in which one group asks them to inspire another about a change effort. Often, the WLP person is the middleman between two groups—sponsors, who want change, and clients, who are supposed to benefit from a change effort, though the benefits may not be apparent to them. Unfortunately, they are sometimes handed

the role without any input, with the result that they may not support the choice of the intervention or the methods chosen for implementation. Consider the following vignettes. Decide for yourself how well the change leadership process was handled in each situation.

Vignette 1: In the middle of a change effort to install teams in an organization, the manager of a department states, "It is puzzling to me why we began this change effort. What are we supposed to get out of it?"

Vignette 2: An employee in a process improvement meeting says, "I am not enthusiastic about these process improvement efforts. This year my raise was way below what it should have been. Why should I help the company do better when the company does not seem to care about me?"

Vignette 3: During the installation of a team-based management program in which supervisors are being replaced by self-directed work teams, a former supervisor says, "You know, I long for the days when I could just order people to do things. Now I have to work with and through others, convincing them and influencing them. That takes so much time. I am exhausted at the end of a workday."

As you continue reading about the change leader's role, think about these vignettes. What should a change leader do in these and similar situations?

When Initiated by the Change Leader. Although WLP practitioners are often prompted to enact the role of change leader in response to requests by others, WLP practitioners also have an obligation to be proactive—that is, to build enthusiasm about interventions even when they are not requested by others to do so. In these situations they are said to initiate the role of change leader.

WLP practitioners who initiate change leadership on their own, just like those who initiate analysis or evaluation on their own, face a greater challenge than those who simply react to the requests of others. Nobody has asked for their opinion or recommendations. Superficial comments like "things are going well" may prompt a flood of complaints and produce exactly the opposite of genuine enthusiasm. And sometimes stakeholders view such efforts as mere grandstanding on the part of self-interested WLP practitioners who want to justify their existence. Just like analysts or evaluators who act proactively, change leaders must first find a sponsor or change champion to build awareness of the value of the intervention and track results. A change champion can help the change leader to demonstrate that a change effort has produced verifiable business results, above and beyond so-called cheerleading efforts such as sales slogans and banners.

What Projects Do Change Leaders Carry Out?

Change leaders may independently make recommendations about what methods should be used to make others enthusiastic about interventions, why those interventions are appropriate, how the interventions will benefit (or have benefited) workers and the organization, and what results should be expected from the interventions and when they should be expected. Alternatively, change leaders may serve as facilitators for task forces, project teams, or other groups from an organization that is formed to build awareness and enthusiasm for interventions and communicate results. Change leadership projects, like analysis or evaluation projects, can range in scope from the small scale to the large scale. Projects can also be carried out as isolated and stand-alone efforts, or they can be integrated with other efforts. The central question governing scope is this: What is the size of the group that will participate, is participating, or has participated in the intervention?

Many WLP practitioners are familiar with small-scale interventions. Examples might include situations in which managers request help in solving a problem with one worker. In those cases, it may not be possible to communicate about results or inspire others, beyond recognizing publicly that improvements have occurred. Such projects are often carried out as one step in a process having many steps. But the change leadership role, much like other roles, can also be carried out as large-scale projects. Examples might include situations in which WLP practitioners are asked to participate on a team to improve feedback in the organization, improve incentives and rewards, improve selection methods, and so forth. In each case, change leaders are needed to build awareness of the problem, the intervention undertaken to solve the problem, and the results realized from the intervention as information about those results are available.

SECTION 1   GETTING STARTED

SECTION 2   DEFINING THE ROLES

SECTION 3   ENACTING THE ROLE OF MANAGER

◆ A Model of the Management Process

◆ Steps in the Management Process
— Step 1: Formulate a Vision of WLP for the Organization, Department, or Work Group
— Step 2: Communicate the Vision to Others and Build Their Enthusiasm
— Step 3: Clarify the Goals and Objectives Necessary to Realize the Vision
— Step 4: Clarify the People, Data, and Things Necessary to Realize the Vision
— Step 5: Create and Implement an Action Plan to Align With Organizational and HR Plans
— Step 6: Establish the Policy, Select and Develop People, Organize and Schedule Work Processes, Assign Responsibility, and Lead the Work
— Step 7: Establish and Maintain a Work Climate That Is Conducive to Realizing the Vision and Implementing the Action Plan
— Step 8: Develop a Follow-Up and Monitoring System to Track Results Against Intentions
— Step 9: Establish and Implement a Communication Strategy and Plan to Build Enthusiasm for WLP Initiatives
— Step 10: Work With All Necessary Stakeholder Groups to Ensure Continuous Improvement of WLP Efforts

◆ Section Summary

SECTION 4   ENACTING THE ROLE OF CHANGE LEADER

SECTION 5   TOOLS FOR CONDUCTING MANAGEMENT AND CHANGE LEADERSHIP

SECTION 6   AFTERWORD

SECTION 7   BIBLIOGRAPHY

The manager role "plans, organizes, schedules, monitors, and leads the work of individuals and groups to attain desired results; facilitates the strategic plan; ensures that workplace learning and performance is aligned with organizational needs and plans; and ensures accomplishment of the administrative requirements of the function" (Rothwell, Sanders, and Soper, 1999, p. 43). When WLP practitioners or others enact this role, they oversee WLP in an organization, department, function, or work unit. They may also oversee WLP during a project, such as an intervention designed to improve company selection methods, reward systems, ergonomic use of tools or equipment, or other performance enhancement efforts. The key to effective management of WLP is to take a holistic, strategic perspective that goes beyond solving isolated performance problems to finding leverage for quantum-leap improvements of entire systems, subsystems, and organizations (Hill and Brethower, 1997). Managers of WLP focus their attention on overall organization performance—often with a special focus on organizational processes, policies, procedures, and resources while connecting individual and organizational goals (Adler and Swiercz, 1997).

A *model* helps describe or clarify an otherwise complex object or process. Model building is as important in management as it is in other roles of the WLP practitioner. A management process model helps WLP practitioners and other people carry out effective management of WLP. Each step in the model requires action to be taken.

A Model of the Management Process

One way to think of the management process is as a series of general steps as follows:

1. Formulate a vision of WLP for the organization, department, or work group.

2. Communicate the vision to others and build their enthusiasm.

3. Clarify the goals and objectives necessary to realize the vision.

4. Clarify the people, data, and things necessary to realize the vision.

5. Create and implement an action plan and align it with organizational and HR plans.

6. Establish the policy, select and develop people, organize and schedule work processes, assign responsibility, and lead the work.

7. Establish and maintain a work climate that is conducive to realizing the vision and implementing the action plan.

8. Develop a follow-up and monitoring system to track results against intentions.

9. Establish and implement a communication strategy and plan to build enthusiasm for WLP initiatives.

10. Work with all necessary stakeholder groups to ensure continuous improvement of WLP efforts.

These steps are depicted in figure 3.1, and their relationship to the manager of WLP's competencies are depicted in table 3.1. This section addresses these steps and provides guidance for applying them. As you think about managing WLP, use figure 5.1, "Worksheet to Guide the Management of WLP," on page 94 to help pose questions related to each step of the model.

Step 1:
Formulate a Vision of WLP for the Organization, Department,
or Work Group

Step 2:
Communicate the Vision to Others and Build Their Enthusiasm

Step 3:
Clarify the Goals and Objectives Necessary to Realize the Vision

Step 4:
Clarify the People, Data, and Things Necessary to Realize the Vision

Step 5:
Create and Implement an Action Plan and Align It With
the Organizational and HR Plans

Step 6:
Establish the Policy, Select and Develop People, Organize and Schedule
Work Processes, Assign Responsibility, and Lead the Work

Step 7:
Establish and Maintain a Work Climate That Is Conducive to
Realizing the Vision and Implementing the Action Plan

Step 8:
Develop a Follow-Up and Monitoring System to
Track Results Against Intentions

Step 9:
Establish and Implement a Communication Strategy and
Plan to Build Enthusiasm for WLP Initiatives

Step 10:
Work With All Necessary Stakeholder Groups to Ensure
Continuous Improvement of WLP Efforts

Table 3.1: Relationship Between the Management Process and the Competencies of the Manager of WLP*

Model of Management	Competencies of the Manager of WLP
Formulate a Vision of WLP for the Organization, Department, or Work Group	♦ *Ability to see the big picture:* Identifying trends and patterns that are outside the normal paradigm of the organization. ♦ *Analytical thinking:* Clarifying complex issues by breaking them down into meaningful components and synthesizing related items. ♦ *Business knowledge:* Demonstrating awareness of business functions and how business decisions affect financial and nonfinancial work results. ♦ *Buy-in advocacy:* Building ownership and support for workplace initiatives. ♦ *Communication:* Applying effective verbal, nonverbal, and written communication methods to achieve desired results. ♦ *Communication networks:* Understanding the various methods through which communication is achieved. ♦ *Consulting:* Understanding the results that stakeholders desire from a process and providing insight into how they can best use their resources to achieve goals. ♦ *Cost-benefit analysis:* Accurately assessing the relative value of performance improvement interventions. ♦ *Diversity awareness:* Assessing the impact and appropriateness of interventions on individuals, groups, and organizations. ♦ *Evaluation of results against organizational goals:* Assessing how well workplace performance, learning strategies, and results match organizational goals and strategic intent. ♦ *Facilitation:* Helping others to discover new insights. ♦ *Feedback:* Providing performance information to the appropriate people. ♦ *Group dynamics:* Assessing how groups of people function and evolve as they seek to meet the needs of their members and of the organization. ♦ *Identification of critical business issues:* Determining key business issues and forces for change and applying that knowledge to performance improvement strategies. ♦ *Industry awareness:* Understanding the current and future climate of the organization's industry and formulating strategies that respond to that climate. ♦ *Interpersonal relationship building:* Effectively interacting with others in order to produce meaningful outcomes. ♦ *Knowledge capital:* Measuring knowledge capital and determining its value to the organization. ♦ *Leadership:* Leading, influencing, and coaching others to help them achieve desired results. ♦ *Negotiating and contracting:* Organizing, preparing, monitoring, and evaluating work performed by vendors and consultants. ♦ *Organization development theory and application:* Understanding the theories, techniques, and appropriate applications of organization development interventions as they are used for performance improvement. ♦ *Outsourcing management:* Ability to identify and select specialized resources outside of the organization; identifying, selecting, and managing technical specifications for these specialized resources. ♦ *Performance gap analysis:* Performing front-end analysis by comparing actual and ideal performance levels in the workplace; identifying opportunities and strategies for performance improvement. ♦ *Performance theory:* Recognizing the implications, outcomes, and consequences of performance interventions to distinguish between activities and results.

(continued on next page)

*Some competencies are used in more than one step of the model.

Table 3.1: Relationship Between the Management Process and the Competencies of the Manager of WLP *(continued)*

Model of Management	Competencies of the Manager of WLP
Formulate a Vision of WLP for the Organization, Department, or Work Group *(continued)*	♦ *Process consultation:* Using a monitoring and feedback method to continually improve the productivity of work groups. ♦ *Quality implications:* Identifying the relationships and implications of quality programs and performance. ♦ *Reward system theory and application:* Understanding the theories, techniques, and appropriate applications of reward system interventions used for performance improvement. ♦ *Social awareness:* Seeing organizations as dynamic political, economic, and social systems. ♦ *Standards identification:* Determining what constitutes success for individuals, organizations, and processes. ♦ *Systems thinking:* Recognizing the interrelationship among events by determining the driving forces that connect seemingly isolated incidents within the organization; taking a holistic view of performance problems in order to find root causes. ♦ *Visioning:* Seeing the possibilities of what can be and inspiring a shared sense of purpose within the organization. ♦ *Work environment analysis:* Examining the work environment for issues or characteristics that affect human performance; understanding characteristics of a high-performance workplace.
Communicate the Vision to Others and Build Their Enthusiasm	♦ *Buy-in advocacy:* Building ownership and support for workplace initiatives. ♦ *Communication:* Applying effective verbal, nonverbal, and written communication methods to achieve desired results. ♦ *Communication networks:* Understanding the various methods through which communication is achieved. ♦ *Diversity awareness:* Assessing the impact and appropriateness of interventions on individuals, groups, and organizations. ♦ *Interpersonal relationship building:* Effectively interacting with others in order to produce meaningful outcomes.
Clarify the Goals and Objectives Necessary to Realize the Vision	♦ *Ability to see the big picture:* Identifying trends and patterns that are outside the normal paradigm of the organization. ♦ *Analytical thinking:* Clarifying complex issues by breaking them down into meaningful components and synthesizing related items. ♦ *Business knowledge:* Demonstrating awareness of business functions and how business decisions affect financial and nonfinancial work results. ♦ *Competency identification:* Identifying the skills, knowledge, and attitudes required to perform work. ♦ *Cost-benefit analysis:* Accurately assessing the relative value of performance improvement interventions. ♦ *Ethics modeling:* Modeling exemplary ethical behavior and understanding the implications of this responsibility.

Model of Management	Competencies of the Manager of WLP

Clarify the Goals and Objectives Necessary to Realize the Vision
(continued)

♦ *Evaluation of results against organizational goals:* Assessing how well workplace performance, learning strategies, and results match organizational goals and strategic intent.

♦ *Facilitation:* Helping others to discover new insights.

♦ *Feedback:* Providing performance information to the appropriate people.

♦ *Group dynamics:* Assessing how groups of people function and evolve as they seek to meet the needs of their members and of the organization.

♦ *Identification of critical business issues:* Determining key business issues and forces for change and applying that knowledge to performance improvement strategies.

♦ *Industry awareness:* Understanding the current and future climate of the organization's industry and formulating strategies that respond to that climate.

♦ *Knowledge capital:* Measuring knowledge capital and determining its value to the organization.

♦ *Knowledge management:* Developing and implementing systems for creating, managing, and distributing knowledge.

♦ *Leadership:* Leading, influencing, and coaching others to help them achieve desired results.

♦ *Negotiating and contracting:* Organizing, preparing, monitoring, and evaluating work performed by vendors and consultants.

♦ *Organization development theory and application:* Understanding the theories, techniques, and appropriate applications of organization development interventions as they are used for performance improvement.

♦ *Outsourcing management:* Ability to identify and select specialized resources outside of the organization; identifying, selecting, and managing technical specifications for these specialized resources.

♦ *Performance theory:* Recognizing the implications, outcomes, and consequences of performance interventions to distinguish between activities and results.

♦ *Reward system theory and application:* Understanding the theories, techniques, and appropriate applications of reward system interventions used for performance improvement.

♦ *Social awareness:* Seeing organizations as dynamic political, economic, and social systems.

♦ *Standards identification:* Determining what constitutes success for individuals, organizations, and processes.

♦ *Systems thinking:* Recognizing the interrelationship among events by determining the driving forces that connect seemingly isolated incidents within the organization; taking a holistic view of performance problems in order to find root causes.

♦ *Visioning:* Seeing the possibilities of what can be and inspiring a shared sense of purpose within the organization.

♦ *Work environment analysis:* Examining the work environment for issues or characteristics that affect human performance; understanding characteristics of a high-performance workplace.

(continued on next page)

Model of Management	Competencies of the Manager of WLP
Clarify the People, Data, and Things Necessary to Realize the Vision	◆ *Analytical thinking:* Clarifying complex issues by breaking them down into meaningful components and synthesizing related items. ◆ *Business knowledge:* Demonstrating awareness of business functions and how business decisions affect financial and nonfinancial work results. ◆ *Buy-in advocacy:* Building ownership and support for workplace initiatives. ◆ *Coping skills:* Dealing with ambiguity and stress resulting from conflicting information and goals; helping others deal with ambiguity and stress. ◆ *Cost-benefit analysis:* Accurately assessing the relative value of performance improvement interventions. ◆ *Group dynamics:* Assessing how groups of people function and evolve as they seek to meet the needs of their members and of the organization. ◆ *Interpersonal relationship building:* Effectively interacting with others in order to produce meaningful outcomes. ◆ *Leadership:* Leading, influencing, and coaching others to help them achieve desired results. ◆ *Negotiating and contracting:* Organizing, preparing, monitoring, and evaluating work performed by vendors and consultants. ◆ *Outsourcing management:* Ability to identify and select specialized resources outside of the organization; identifying, selecting, and managing technical specifications for these specialized resources. ◆ *Project management:* Planning, organizing, and monitoring work. ◆ *Quality implications:* Identifying the relationships and implications of quality programs and performance. ◆ *Social awareness:* Seeing organizations as dynamic political, economic, and social systems. ◆ *Staff selection theory and application:* Understanding the theories, techniques, and appropriate applications of staff selection interventions used for performance improvement. ◆ *Standards identification:* Determining what constitutes success for individuals, organizations, and processes. ◆ *Systems thinking:* Recognizing the interrelationship among events by determining the driving forces that connect seemingly isolated incidents within the organization; taking a holistic view of performance problems in order to find root causes. ◆ *Work environment analysis:* Examining the work environment for issues or characteristics that affect human performance; understanding characteristics of a high-performance workplace.
Create and Implement an Action Plan and Align It with Organizational and HR Plans	◆ *Buy-in advocacy:* Building ownership and support for workplace initiatives. ◆ *Computer-mediated communication:* Understanding the implication of current and evolving computer-based electronic communication. ◆ *Consulting:* Understanding the results that stakeholders desire from a process and providing insight into how they can best use their resources to achieve goals. ◆ *Coping skills:* Dealing with ambiguity and stress resulting from conflicting information and goals; helping others deal with ambiguity and stress. ◆ *Cost-benefit analysis:* Accurately assessing the relative value of performance improvement interventions.

Model of Management	Competencies of the Manager of WLP
Create and Implement an Action Plan and Align It with Organizational and HR Plans (*continued*)	◆ *Diversity awareness:* Assessing the impact and appropriateness of interventions on individuals, groups, and organizations. ◆ *Identification of critical business issues:* Determining key business issues and forces for change and applying that knowledge to performance improvement strategies. ◆ *Industry awareness:* Understanding the current and future climate of the organization's industry and formulating strategies that respond to that climate. ◆ *Interpersonal relationship building:* Effectively interacting with others in order to produce meaningful outcomes. ◆ *Leadership:* Leading, influencing, and coaching others to help them achieve desired results. ◆ *Negotiating and contracting:* Organizing, preparing, monitoring, and evaluating work performed by vendors and consultants. ◆ *Outsourcing management:* Ability to identify and select specialized resources outside of the organization; identifying, selecting, and managing technical specifications for these specialized resources. ◆ *Project management:* Planning, organizing, and monitoring work. ◆ *Quality implications:* Identifying the relationships and implications of quality programs and performance. ◆ *Technological literacy:* Understanding and appropriately applying existing, new, or emerging technology. ◆ *Visioning:* Seeing the possibilities of what can be and inspiring a shared sense of purpose within the organization.
Establish the Policy, Select and Develop People, Organize and Schedule Work Processes, Assign Responsibility, and Lead the Work	◆ *Buy-in advocacy:* Building ownership and support for workplace initiatives. ◆ *Communication:* Applying effective verbal, nonverbal, and written communication methods to achieve desired results. ◆ *Communication networks:* Understanding the various methods through which communication is achieved. ◆ *Computer-mediated communication:* Understanding the implication of current and evolving computer-based electronic communication. ◆ *Consulting:* Understanding the results that stakeholders desire from a process and providing insight into how they can best use their resources to achieve goals. ◆ *Coping skills:* Dealing with ambiguity and stress resulting from conflicting information and goals; helping others deal with ambiguity and stress. ◆ *Diversity awareness:* Assessing the impact and appropriateness of interventions on individuals, groups, and organizations. ◆ *Ethics modeling:* Modeling exemplary ethical behavior and understanding the implications of this responsibility. ◆ *Facilitation:* Helping others to discover new insights. ◆ *Feedback:* Providing performance information to the appropriate people. ◆ *Group dynamics:* Assessing how groups of people function and evolve as they seek to meet the needs of their members and of the organization. ◆ *Interpersonal relationship building:* Effectively interacting with others in order to produce meaningful outcomes. ◆ *Knowledge management:* Developing and implementing systems for creating, managing, and distributing knowledge. ◆ *Leadership:* Leading, influencing, and coaching others to help them achieve desired results.

(*continued on next page*)

Model of Management	Competencies of the Manager of WLP
Establish the Policy, Select and Develop People, Organize and Schedule Work Processes, Assign Responsibility, and Lead the Work *(continued)*	◆ *Negotiating and contracting:* Organizing, preparing, monitoring, and evaluating work performed by vendors and consultants. ◆ *Organization development theory and application:* Understanding the theories, techniques, and appropriate applications of organization development interventions as they are used for performance improvement. ◆ *Outsourcing management:* Ability to identify and select specialized resources outside of the organization; identifying, selecting, and managing technical specifications for these specialized resources. ◆ *Process consultation:* Using a monitoring and feedback method to continually improve the productivity of work groups. ◆ *Project management:* Planning, organizing, and monitoring work. ◆ *Quality implications:* Identifying the relationships and implications of quality programs and performance. ◆ *Reward system theory and application:* Understanding the theories, techniques, and appropriate applications of reward system interventions used for performance improvement. ◆ *Social awareness:* Seeing organizations as dynamic political, economic, and social systems. ◆ *Staff selection theory and application:* Understanding the theories, techniques, and appropriate applications of staff selection interventions used for performance improvement. ◆ *Standards identification:* Determining what constitutes success for individuals, organizations, and processes. ◆ *Systems thinking:* Recognizing the interrelationship among events by determining the driving forces that connect seemingly isolated incidents within the organization; taking a holistic view of performance problems in order to find root causes. ◆ *Technological literacy:* Understanding and appropriately applying existing, new, or emerging technology. ◆ *Visioning:* Seeing the possibilities of what can be and inspiring a shared sense of purpose within the organization. ◆ *Work environment analysis:* Examining the work environment for issues or characteristics that affect human performance; understanding characteristics of a high-performance workplace.
Establish and Maintain a Work Climate That Is Conducive to Realizing the Vision and Implementing the Action Plan	◆ *Ability to see the big picture:* Identifying trends and patterns that are outside the normal paradigm of the organization. ◆ *Business knowledge:* Demonstrating awareness of business functions and how business decisions affect financial and nonfinancial work results. ◆ *Career development theory and application:* Understanding the theories, techniques, and appropriate applications of career development interventions used for performance improvement. ◆ *Competency identification:* Identifying the skills, knowledge, and attitudes required to perform work. ◆ *Identification of critical business issues:* Determining key business issues and forces for change and applying that knowledge to performance improvement strategies. ◆ *Knowledge management:* Developing and implementing systems for creating, managing, and distributing knowledge.

Model of Management	Competencies of the Manager of WLP

Establish and Maintain a Work Climate That Is Conducive to Realizing the Vision and Implementing the Action Plan
(continued)

♦ *Negotiating and contracting:* Organizing, preparing, monitoring, and evaluating work performed by vendors and consultants.

♦ *Organization development theory and application:* Understanding the theories, techniques, and appropriate applications of organization development interventions as they are used for performance improvement.

♦ *Process consultation:* Using a monitoring and feedback method to continually improve the productivity of work groups.

♦ *Reward system theory and application:* Understanding the theories, techniques, and appropriate applications of reward system interventions used for performance improvement.

♦ *Social awareness:* Seeing organizations as dynamic political, economic, and social systems.

♦ *Staff selection theory and application:* Understanding the theories, techniques, and appropriate applications of staff selection interventions used for performance improvement.

♦ *Standards identification:* Determining what constitutes success for individuals, organizations, and processes.

♦ *Systems thinking:* Recognizing the interrelationship among events by determining the driving forces that connect seemingly isolated incidents within the organization; taking a holistic view of performance problems in order to find root causes.

♦ *Work environment analysis:* Examining the work environment for issues or characteristics that affect human performance; understanding characteristics of a high-performance workplace.

Develop a Follow-Up and Monitoring System to Track Results Against Intentions

♦ *Ability to see the big picture:* Identifying trends and patterns that are outside the normal paradigm of the organization.

♦ *Analytical thinking:* Clarifying complex issues by breaking them down into meaningful components and synthesizing related items.

♦ *Business knowledge:* Demonstrating awareness of business functions and how business decisions affect financial and nonfinancial work results.

♦ *Buy-in advocacy:* Building ownership and support for workplace initiatives.

♦ *Communication:* Applying effective verbal, nonverbal, and written communication methods to achieve desired results.

♦ *Communication networks:* Understanding the various methods through which communication is achieved.

♦ *Computer-mediated communication:* Understanding the implication of current and evolving computer-based electronic communication.

♦ *Consulting:* Understanding the results that stakeholders desire from a process and providing insight into how they can best use their resources to achieve goals.

♦ *Cost-benefit analysis:* Accurately assessing the relative value of performance improvement interventions.

♦ *Diversity awareness:* Assessing the impact and appropriateness of interventions on individuals, groups, and organizations.

♦ *Evaluation of results against organizational goals:* Assessing how well workplace performance, learning strategies, and results match organizational goals and strategic intent.

(continued on next page)

Model of Management	Competencies of the Manager of WLP
Develop a Follow-Up and Monitoring System to Track Results Against Intentions *(continued)*	◆ *Feedback:* Providing performance information to the appropriate people. ◆ *Group dynamics:* Assessing how groups of people function and evolve as they seek to meet the needs of their members and of the organization. ◆ *Identification of critical business issues:* Determining key business issues and forces for change and applying that knowledge to performance improvement strategies. ◆ *Interpersonal relationship building:* Effectively interacting with others in order to produce meaningful outcomes. ◆ *Knowledge capital:* Measuring knowledge capital and determining its value to the organization. ◆ *Knowledge management:* Developing and implementing systems for creating, managing, and distributing knowledge. ◆ *Performance gap analysis:* Performing front-end analysis by comparing actual and ideal performance levels in the workplace; identifying opportunities and strategies for performance improvement. ◆ *Performance theory:* Recognizing the implications, outcomes, and consequences of performance interventions to distinguish between activities and results. ◆ *Process consultation:* Using a monitoring and feedback method to continually improve the productivity of work groups. ◆ *Social awareness:* Seeing organizations as dynamic political, economic, and social systems. ◆ *Technological literacy:* Understanding and appropriately applying existing, new, or emerging technology.
Establish and Implement a Communication Strategy and Plan to Build Enthusiasm for WLP Initiatives	◆ *Ability to see the big picture:* Identifying trends and patterns that are outside the normal paradigm of the organization. ◆ *Business knowledge:* Demonstrating awareness of business functions and how business decisions affect financial and nonfinancial work results. ◆ *Buy-in advocacy:* Building ownership and support for workplace initiatives. ◆ *Communication:* Applying effective verbal, nonverbal, and written communication methods to achieve desired results. ◆ *Communication networks:* Understanding the various methods through which communication is achieved. ◆ *Computer-mediated communication:* Understanding the implication of current and evolving computer-based electronic communication. ◆ *Consulting:* Understanding the results that stakeholders desire from a process and providing insight into how they can best use their resources to achieve goals. ◆ *Cost-benefit analysis:* Accurately assessing the relative value of performance improvement interventions. ◆ *Diversity awareness:* Assessing the impact and appropriateness of interventions on individuals, groups, and organizations. ◆ *Evaluation of results against organizational goals:* Assessing how well workplace performance, learning strategies, and results match organizational goals and strategic intent. ◆ *Feedback:* Providing performance information to the appropriate people. ◆ *Group dynamics:* Assessing how groups of people function and evolve as they seek to meet the needs of their members and of the organization.

Model of Management	Competencies of the Manager of WLP

Establish and Implement a Communication Strategy and Plan to Build Enthusiasm for WLP Initiatives *(continued)*

- *Identification of critical business issues:* Determining key business issues and forces for change and applying that knowledge to performance improvement strategies.
- *Industry awareness:* Understanding the current and future climate of the organization's industry and formulating strategies that respond to that climate.
- *Interpersonal relationship building:* Effectively interacting with others in order to produce meaningful outcomes.
- *Knowledge capital:* Measuring knowledge capital and determining its value to the organization.
- *Leadership:* Leading, influencing, and coaching others to help them achieve desired results.
- *Quality implications:* Identifying the relationships and implications of quality programs and performance.
- *Performance theory:* Recognizing the implications, outcomes, and consequences of performance interventions to distinguish between activities and results.
- *Process consultation:* Using a monitoring and feedback method to continually improve the productivity of work groups.
- *Social awareness:* Seeing organizations as dynamic political, economic, and social systems.
- *Standards identification:* Determining what constitutes success for individuals, organizations, and processes.
- *Technological literacy:* Understanding and appropriately applying existing, new, or emerging technology.
- *Work environment analysis:* Examining the work environment for issues or characteristics that affect human performance; understanding characteristics of a high-performance workplace.

Works With All Necessary Stakeholder Groups to Ensure Continuous Improvement of WLP Efforts

- *Ability to see the big picture:* Identifying trends and patterns that are outside the normal paradigm of the organization.
- *Business knowledge:* Demonstrating awareness of business functions and how business decisions affect financial and nonfinancial work results.
- *Buy-in advocacy:* Building ownership and support for workplace initiatives.
- *Communication:* Applying effective verbal, nonverbal, and written communication methods to achieve desired results.
- *Communication networks:* Understanding the various methods through which communication is achieved.
- *Consulting:* Understanding the results that stakeholders desire from a process and providing insight into how they can best use their resources to achieve goals.
- *Diversity awareness:* Assessing the impact and appropriateness of interventions on individuals, groups, and organizations.
- *Ethics modeling:* Modeling exemplary ethical behavior and understanding the implications of this responsibility.
- *Group dynamics:* Assessing how groups of people function and evolve as they seek to meet the needs of their members and of the organization.
- *Interpersonal relationship building:* Effectively interacting with others in order to produce meaningful outcomes.

(continued on next page)

Table 3.1: Relationship Between the Management Process and the Competencies of the Manager of WLP (*continued*)

Model of Management	Competencies of the Manager of WLP
Work With All Necessary Stakeholder Groups to Ensure Continuous Improvement of WLP Efforts (*continued*)	◆ *Social awareness:* Seeing organizations as dynamic political, economic, and social systems. ◆ *Standards identification:* Determining what constitutes success for individuals, organizations, and processes. ◆ *Work environment analysis:* Examining the work environment for issues or characteristics that affect human performance; understanding characteristics of a high-performance workplace.

Steps in the Management Process

Each step of the management process is treated in a similar way. The definition and purpose of the step is explained, then notes about implementing the step are given, and finally, there is an example that dramatizes what the step can mean in practice.

Step 1: Formulate a Vision of WLP for the Organization, Department, or Work Group

Definition and Purpose of Step 1

In cooperation with key stakeholders, management would formulate a vision of WLP for the organization, department, or work group to help it achieve the organization's strategic objectives, address business issues, seize improvement opportunities, and solve business problems. Begin management of WLP by creating a vision of what it should look like and how it should be managed in the organization. That means deciding what spots in the organization would lead to the greatest performance impact if they were addressed first. The choices facing management are comparable to those of a diamond cutter who is choosing where and how to cut the gem to save the most material and uncover the greatest beauty. (See figure 3.2.)

An important reason to begin with this step is that it is essential to have a sense of the purpose or mission of the WLP function, and a vision of what role WLP should play in the organization is a necessary preliminary step to establishing a purpose or mission statement for WLP in the organization. Without a vision, the WLP department, function, or effort is in danger of trying to be all things to all people—with the result that it will be nothing to anyone.

A vision is an image of what the WLP function should look like in the organization, what role it should play, and what results it should realize. There are many ways that WLP can contribute to an organization. These include the following:

◆ Reduce the otherwise unproductive breaking-in period of new hires.

◆ Improve the socialization of new workers.

◆ Improve the performance of existing workers.

◆ Prepare workers for changes before they happen or during the change.

◆ Solve specific problems with individual, group, or organizational performance.

◆ Find new opportunities for performance improvement.

A vision provides an image of what role the WLP function should play in these and other efforts. To create a vision for WLP, pose questions like these to stakeholders:

◆ Who should bear responsibility for WLP, and who should WLP primarily serve?

◆ What should be the role of WLP in the organization, and why should it enact that role?

◆ When should WLP be a key focus of attention in the organization, and why is that appropriate?

◆ Where—that is, in what geographical locations or in what part of the organization—should WLP be centered?

◆ Why should the organization sponsor WLP, and what results should be sought from it?

◆ How should WLP be carried out in the organization?

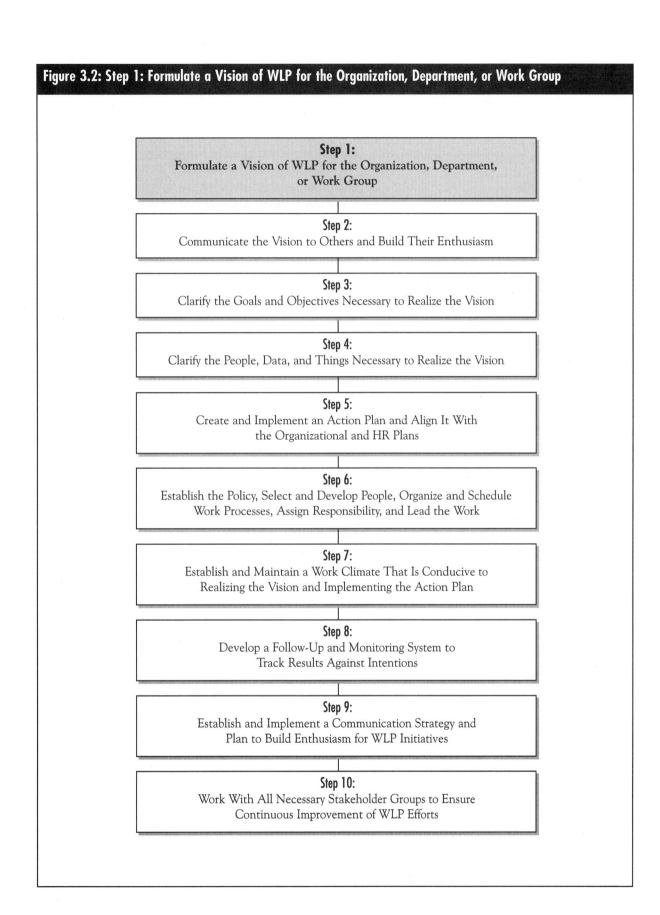

Step 1:
Formulate a Vision of WLP for the Organization, Department, or Work Group

Step 2:
Communicate the Vision to Others and Build Their Enthusiasm

Step 3:
Clarify the Goals and Objectives Necessary to Realize the Vision

Step 4:
Clarify the People, Data, and Things Necessary to Realize the Vision

Step 5:
Create and Implement an Action Plan and Align It With the Organizational and HR Plans

Step 6:
Establish the Policy, Select and Develop People, Organize and Schedule Work Processes, Assign Responsibility, and Lead the Work

Step 7:
Establish and Maintain a Work Climate That Is Conducive to Realizing the Vision and Implementing the Action Plan

Step 8:
Develop a Follow-Up and Monitoring System to Track Results Against Intentions

Step 9:
Establish and Implement a Communication Strategy and Plan to Build Enthusiasm for WLP Initiatives

Step 10:
Work With All Necessary Stakeholder Groups to Ensure Continuous Improvement of WLP Efforts

How much should WLP contribute to the organization, and how should its results be assessed, tracked, and communicated?

Creating and sustaining a vision involves clarifying these points and communicating them to key groups inside and outside the organization. Many organizations have achieved benefits from sharing their vision statements with employees (Grensing-Pophal, 2000). According to Lee (1993, p. 26), "the concept of vision has never been more important than in today's world of flattened, delayered, decentralized organizations."

WLP in most organizations is shaped, to a considerable extent, by the needs of the organization as they are perceived through the values of senior managers. Examples of real or perceived needs include any of the following reasons:

♦ Turnover is perceived to be extraordinarily high.

♦ Workers need improved socialization.

♦ Training is handled informally and is not well organized.

♦ Training is required to help workers adapt to new technology or competitive conditions.

♦ Training is necessary to help individuals prepare for advancement.

Alternatively, senior managers in organizations value workers and believe that workplace learning has an impact on performance.

The first step in managing WLP is to formulate a vision of WLP. That should not be done in isolation or by one person alone. If it is, it is not likely to gain much support from key decision makers or stakeholders. Instead, visioning should be carried out in a process that involves those who stand to benefit from the WLP effort. That may include representatives of management, organized labor, workers, and, if WLP serves other groups, representatives of such other stakeholders as customers, members of the community, company suppliers, company distributors, and company wholesalers. (For one way to do that, see figure 3.3.)

Implementing Step 1

Much has been written about how to go about the visioning process (see, for instance, Ackoff, 1993; Allen, 1995; Finaly, 1994; Latham, 1995).

But one way to establish a vision for the WLP effort in the organization, department, or work unit is by interviewing key stakeholders individually and holding focus groups collectively to gather information about what others desire from WLP. If necessary, identify best practice WLP efforts in the industry and organize a field trip to see them firsthand. Use Step 1 of the worksheet in figure 5.1 to pose the questions listed in the section above to stakeholders to determine what vision others may have for WLP in the organization, department, or work group. If you wish, poll stakeholders on these and related issues by using the survey questionnaire in figure 3.4. While it is important to build agreement by pinpointing common desires, needs and expectations for WLP, it is also important to identify areas of disagreement since they may be more revealing about the values, interests, conflicts, and priorities of different key groups in the organization.

Vignette. The PQR Corporation is an explosive growth company. (Note that names have been changed.) Founded just three years ago, the company has grown from a one-person enterprise that the founding entrepreneur, Norman Richards (now the CEO), conducted from his garage to a company of 690 people at six locations. The company is a manufacturer of heavy equipment that range in size from devices as small as riding lawnmowers to items as large as huge earth-moving equipment. Such firms are not easily founded or maintained at a time when dot-com companies are the darlings of venture capitalists globally. But PQR Corporation entered the heavy manufacturing industry as a result of a most favorable regulatory and safety change that the Occupational Safety and Health Administration enacted and that caught possible competitors off guard. PQR was small and nimble enough to seize the advantage at the outset of the change in the regulatory environment. The demand for the product line manufactured by PQR was instant and immense.

PQR Corporation's case gives proof to the old adage that if you wish to give people a real problem, grant them their greatest wishes. PQR has had embarrassing success and is amazingly profitable, so much so that the company cannot recruit, select, hire, orient, train, or promote people fast enough to keep up with production demands or

Figure 3.3: Assessment for Establishing a Vision for the WLP Department or Effort

Directions: There are many possible reasons to sponsor a WLP effort or to have a WLP department in an organization. Use this assessment to open a dialogue about why it is useful to have a WLP department. Distribute this assessment to decision makers and stakeholders. First, ask each person to write in the space below why it is useful to have a WLP department or function in the organization. Then, ask each stakeholder to rate the importance of each reason for a WLP department or function in the left column below. For each possible reason listed, stakeholders should circle a response in the right column to indicate how much they agree with it. They should use the following scale: 1= Not applicable; 2 = Strongly disagree; 3 = Disagree; 4 = Agree; 5 = Strongly agree. When the stakeholders are finished, ask them to turn in their assessments. Compile the results and give them feedback on how they rated possible purposes for the WLP department. Use any differences that exist as a way to begin a dialogue to seek clarity and agreement on the purpose of the WLP department or function.

Why is it useful to have a WLP department or function in the organization?

	Possible Purpose of the WLP Department or Function	How Much Do You Agree?				
	I believe that the most important purpose of the WLP department or function is to:	Not Applicable	Strongly Disagree	Disagree	Agree	Strongly Agree
1	Reduce the otherwise unproductive breaking-in period of new hires	1	2	3	4	5
2	Improve the socialization of new workers	1	2	3	4	5
3	Improve the performance of existing workers	1	2	3	4	5
4	Prepare workers for changes before they happen or during the change	1	2	3	4	5
5	Solve specific problems with individual, group, or organizational performance	1	2	3	4	5
6	Find new opportunities for performance improvement	1	2	3	4	5
7	Other (please specify):					

Directions: This instrument is designed to gauge your opinions about a guiding vision or purpose for the WLP department or function. A draft vision statement for the WLP department is provided in the space below. Think about the vision as it is described. Then, rate your opinion of each statement appearing in the left column below. Circle a code in the right column to indicate your level of agreement. Use the following scale: 1= Strongly disagree; 2 = Disagree; 3 = Agree; 4 = Strongly agree. When you finish scoring the instrument, hand it to the designated person. The instrument will serve as a starting point for opening an organized dialogue about the WLP function.

Draft vision statement for WLP in the organization:

Now, rate your agreement with each of the following statements as they apply to the vision for the WLP department, function, or effort in your organization.	Strongly Disagree			Strongly Agree
How Much Do You Agree With Each Statement?	1	2	3	4
1 I think the vision statement does an outstanding job of concisely stating the desired or desirable purpose of the WLP function in this organization.	1	2	3	4
2 I think almost everyone would agree with this statement of the vision for WLP in this organization.	1	2	3	4
3 I think the need for WLP in this organization is apparent.	1	2	3	4
4 I do not believe that additional language should be provided in the vision statement.	1	2	3	4
5 If additional language were to be added to the vision statement to clarify the purpose of the WLP department or function in this organization, then I believe that language should read as follows *(insert your own additions here):*				

customer satisfaction. At this writing, product backlogs stand at one year, despite a 24-hour-a-day, seven-day-a-week schedule and enormous amounts of overtime for the company's few experienced workers. Customer satisfaction rates stand at a six on a scale of seven that an external vendor administered to PQR customers, an enviable rating in its industry.

In 1999, PQR hired a vice president of HR from another, more stable manufacturer, and asked her to set up an HR department from scratch. According to the vice president:

> I run like crazy for 12 hours every day, and I am still behind. I am so busy that I do not have time to go to the restroom. We are now hiring about 10 people a week at each location. At that speed of growth, we have trouble getting workers added to the payroll system in a timely manner, let alone properly oriented, socialized, trained to be productive, and upgraded to keep up with product changes and other requirements. In fact, around here, we are growing so fast that we do not have the infrastructure to support the growth. Nothing works. It is not difficult to be a hero in this organization, given the speed at which we operate. Point at something—anything at all—and it needs to be improved. You want a case study in performance improvement? Come here. I dare you. Why? The reason is that everything is going wrong at once. It is not a matter of fixing what is broken. We don't have anything in place to fix, and that's the problem.

The CEO hired an outside consultant, Gregory Miller, to examine the problem of inadequate worker training and other WLP issues. After conducting many interviews and focus groups with managers and workers alike, the consultant wrote in his report:

> Workers receive no training at all in this company. Anybody who walks in the door is almost automatically hired. They are hired on Friday and told to show up for work on Saturday. They are hired so quickly that they do not even know where to go on their first day or who their supervisors are to be. In fact, they have no parking places and, in some cases, no offices or work sites to go to. Despite a dangerous manufacturing work process, production workers are given no safety orientation before being sent to train on the assembly line. But once they arrive at the company, it turns out that the new hires just stand around because the experienced workers

have no time to show them the ropes....The problems do not end there. The company has grown so fast that the supervisors promoted from within have limited experience themselves and received no training on making the transition to supervisors. The story is the same up the ladder. Middle managers are also promoted from within, have limited experience themselves, and have not received training on the role of middle management. Executives were hourly workers just a few months before. These are just a few of the problems. The company has no job descriptions or competency models; pay practices and the company reward systems generally are (in the words of the VP of HR) "held together with a wing and a prayer"; and the company has not run any projections on how many or what kind of people it needs in the future, with the result that a constant hiring mode leads to much unnecessary hiring. *Everything needs to be created or fixed at once.*

The company's top managers agreed with everything in the consultant's report.

Against this backdrop, Miller, the external consultant, advised Norman Richards, the company CEO, to hire a manager of WLP to launch a many-faceted performance improvement effort that would focus on the following needs:

- workforce planning to match production and sales demands
- recruitment efforts
- selection to ensure that those hired possessed sufficient skills to read blueprints, show up for work, and try to learn
- job design so that workers possessed job descriptions
- orientation so that workers received a proper briefing about the company and OSHA-required safety training
- on-the-job training (OJT) to slash the unproductive breaking-in period of new hires
- training, career planning, and other programs to upgrade the skills of supervisors, managers, and executives.

The company hired Edith Johnson, who had experience as a manager of WLP in an electronics plant near PQR Corporation's headquarters. The external consultant advised Richards to spend time with him and the newly hired WLP manager to formulate a vision of the WLP department for the organization.

A company vision was a new concept to the CEO. He asked the consultant if it would not be appropriate just to hand a vision statement to the WLP manager, but the consultant advised him that it was better to wait until the manager was hired and could participate in the visioning process and thereby gain greater commitment to it. The consultant suggested that the CEO hold a top management retreat early on to "get everyone on the same page, begin the process of clarifying the role of this new department, and set some reasonable and early goals and expectations."

To that end, Richards and the consultant organized a one-day retreat at which the company's senior managers would focus on a vision of the WLP department. The retreat was held off site, planned carefully, and based on one-on-one interviews with many workers, supervisors, managers, and executives. Conducting it in such a fast-paced setting was a challenge.

Early ground rules were established: Nobody in attendance was permitted to use cell phones, accept messages, or stray away from the meeting for longer than 10 minutes. The meeting began with the CEO explaining why WLP was so important to the organization and setting some expectations for meeting outcomes. The consultant then gave about a one-hour presentation in which he described how other manufacturing firms had structured the WLP function. He emphasized the importance of establishing a clear vision to guide the WLP department, ensuring participation and ownership from all levels of the organization to meet real business needs and solve business problems, and setting goals for the WLP department that were achievable when everything was needed at once. The consultant presented the results of the interviews he had conducted, prioritized by need for the new department. He then offered a suggested draft vision statement for the WLP department based on the input from the interviews:

> The purpose of the WLP department at PQR Corporation is to meet the needs for improving the competitive performance of PQR Corporation by serving the immediate needs of workers to learn their work responsibilities, keep current on knowledge and skills relevant to their work responsibilities as organizational needs and conditions change, and prepare for future challenges in their

work and in the organization. The WLP department, working in cooperation with the human resources department and other departments at PQR, will establish training programs, employee educational programs, employee development programs, organization development interventions, career planning and development programs, and other programs as needed to improve individual and organizational performance at PQR.

Top managers were divided into small groups and asked to critique, improve, and refine this mission statement and provide a formal small group presentation upon completion. The consultant also provided several top managers with handouts of mission statements from other company's WLP departments that he obtained from benchmarking, from published sources, and from the ASTD-sponsored resource *ASTD Trainer's Toolkit: Mission Statements for HRD* (Olivetti, 1990).

Step 2: Communicate the Vision to Others and Build Their Enthusiasm

Definition and Purpose of Step 2

This step has to do with communicating the vision for WLP in the organization and building the enthusiasm of key stakeholders and stakeholder groups for it. (See figure 3.5.) It is closely akin to the role of change leader, but in this capacity the manager of WLP is communicating the collective vision of WLP in the organization—and clarifying what it is for (and not for)—rather than building enthusiasm for one intervention, as the change leader does. The outcome of this step is a clear mission statement for WLP that describes its purpose, customers, philosophies, and other relevant issues. The outcome is one that key stakeholders perceive to be useful to the organization.

Implementing Step 2

It is possible to communicate the vision of WLP for the organization in many ways, only some of which will be described here. (Use Step 2 of the worksheet in figure 5.1 to consider how to communicate the vision of WLP to others in the organization, department, or work group and build their enthusiasm for it.) Some of the ways to communicate the

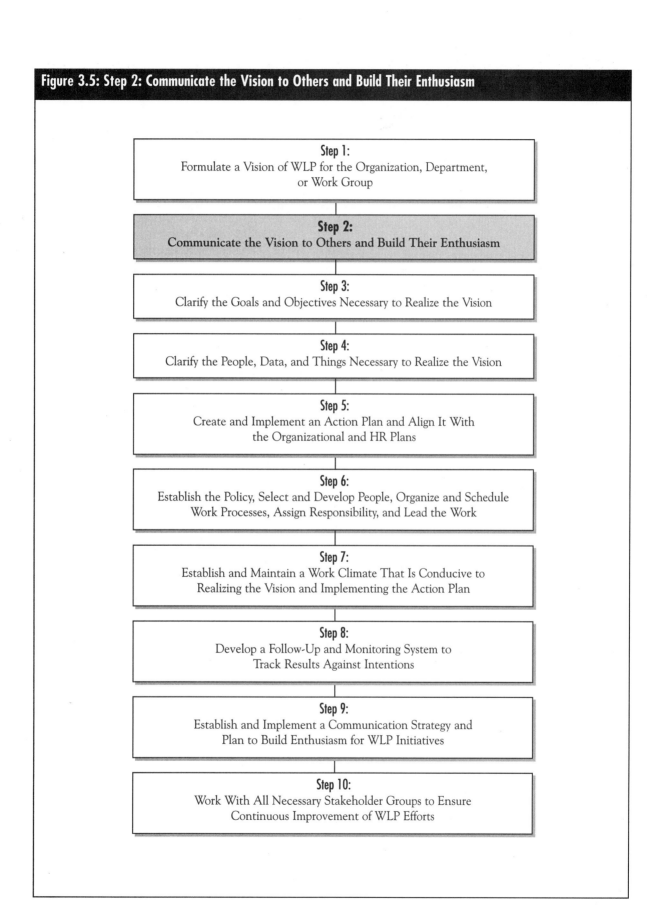

Figure 3.5: Step 2: Communicate the Vision to Others and Build Their Enthusiasm

Step 1:
Formulate a Vision of WLP for the Organization, Department, or Work Group

Step 2:
Communicate the Vision to Others and Build Their Enthusiasm

Step 3:
Clarify the Goals and Objectives Necessary to Realize the Vision

Step 4:
Clarify the People, Data, and Things Necessary to Realize the Vision

Step 5:
Create and Implement an Action Plan and Align It With the Organizational and HR Plans

Step 6:
Establish the Policy, Select and Develop People, Organize and Schedule Work Processes, Assign Responsibility, and Lead the Work

Step 7:
Establish and Maintain a Work Climate That Is Conducive to Realizing the Vision and Implementing the Action Plan

Step 8:
Develop a Follow-Up and Monitoring System to Track Results Against Intentions

Step 9:
Establish and Implement a Communication Strategy and Plan to Build Enthusiasm for WLP Initiatives

Step 10:
Work With All Necessary Stakeholder Groups to Ensure Continuous Improvement of WLP Efforts

vision of the WLP effort and build enthusiasm for it include the following:

♦ Insert a description of the WLP effort into company documents, such as strategic plans, company newsletters, company annual reports, policy and procedure manuals, employee handbooks, and job descriptions. The aim of these communications should be to show how WLP contributes to achieving company strategic objectives as well as to helping employees qualify for their existing jobs, stay current in the face of technological and competitive changes, and prepare for future organizational responsibilities.

♦ Write a company policy on WLP that sets forth its mission or purpose, goals and objectives, company policies and procedures relevant to WLP (such as employee training, employee education, career development efforts, and other learning and nonlearning interventions), and explanations of how WLP helps the organization and its workers achieve improved performance. It is worth stressing that any written policy for WLP should clearly emphasize the business value of WLP efforts, rather than the less-quantifiable value of improving worker morale.

♦ Conduct periodic briefings to management and other stakeholder groups about the organization's WLP efforts. That can be done during regularly scheduled meetings, such as management retreats, staff meetings, or task force meetings. Alternatively, that can be done by hosting receptions in the WLP department or by making thinly veiled sales calls on individual managers and their key reports. The aim of such efforts should always be to explain how WLP can help the organization and its people achieve improved performance.

♦ Conduct information campaigns that resemble sales campaigns. In one large and well-known multinational corporation, for instance, the WLP department prepared a videotape and explanatory booklet that was mailed to all company managers. The video and booklet described the products and services offered by the WLP department and explained when and how to access the WLP department for assistance in solving human performance problems and seizing human performance improvement opportunities.

To consider ways to communicate the vision to others and build their enthusiasm, WLP managers should pose such questions as these to stakeholders:

♦ How can the vision of the WLP effort be most effectively communicated to key stakeholder groups inside and outside the organization?

♦ How can the relative effectiveness of these communication strategies be assessed?

♦ How can the reactions of key stakeholder groups to the vision be organized?

Use the worksheet in figure 3.6 to brainstorm ways to communicate the vision of the WLP effort to others and build their enthusiasm for it.

Vignette: Working with the executive team of PQR Corporation, Gregory Miller, the external consultant, and Edith Johnson, the newly hired WLP manager, focused the first half of the executive retreat on establishing a clear vision and mission statement to guide the newly created WLP department at PQR Corporation. After the small groups of senior executives debriefed their group work, the consultant asked them to summarize key points of agreement and disagreement with the draft mission statement. By using that approach, Miller was able to demonstrate the differences of opinions and expectations among the senior management group, although not all disagreements were ironed out at the retreat.

As a second part of the retreat, Miller asked the senior managers to discuss how the vision for the new WLP department could—and should— be communicated, and he put the ideas on a flip-chart. Suggestions included putting the vision statement for WLP in the company's HR manual, describing it in a newly created orientation program (a first assignment for the new WLP manager), running a feature article in the newly created company newsletter, and placing a description of the vision in the company's annual report.

The vice president of marketing asked why the WLP department was only focused on PQR Corporation employees. He said performance improvement should also be geared to current or prospective company customers, suppliers, distributors, and community members in the communities where PQR Corporation had manufacturing sites. The senior managers discussed that issue at

Figure 3.6: Worksheet for Brainstorming Ways to Communicate the Vision of the WLP Effort and Build Enthusiasm for It

Directions: Use this worksheet to brainstorm some ways to communicate the vision of the WLP department, function, or effort in your organization and build enthusiasm for it. In the column at the left, list some ways to communicate the vision of WLP in your organization. In the column at the right, explain how that vision should be communicated, why the approach you have indicated is a good one, and how you can build enthusiasm for WLP in the organization by using that approach.

	How can you communicate the vision of WLP in your organization?	How should the vision be communicated, why is the approach a good one, and how can you build enthusiasm for WLP by using that approach?
1		
2		
3		
4		
5		
6		

length and eventually agreed that, during the first two years of operation, the WLP department would focus attention on internal training. After that, new programs would be geared to customers.

The vice president of finance asked what the budget for the new department would be and what budget the company was willing to provide for WLP efforts. Miller explained that that question is key, but could not be answered in just a few minutes. He said many companies calculate a percentage of total compensation for training or else mandate a specific number of hours of training per employee per year for training.

Miller asked the senior managers what their role should be in communicating the vision of the WLP department to their departments. They agreed to make it an agenda item for their own upcoming staff meetings. They also agreed to Miller's idea of a standing committee, composed of a cross section of high-potential workers from different hierarchical levels and departments, to draft a company policy on WLP, provide a sounding board for ideas for Johnson, and chair ad hoc committees as needed.

Step 3: Clarify the Goals and Objectives Necessary to Realize the Vision

Definition and Purpose of Step 3

This step pertains to clarifying what results should be obtained from the WLP effort collectively as well as from individual projects. (See figure 3.7.) The goals and objectives should be derived from the vision and the mission or purpose of the WLP effort.

Goals are results to be obtained. They are not time bound or measurable (Rothwell and Kazanas, 1994a, 1994b; Rothwell and Sredl, 2000). Examples of goals include "improving performance," "enhancing customer service," or "building intellectual capital." *Objectives* are derived from goals but are more specific (Rothwell and Kazanas, 1994a, 1994b; Rothwell and Sredl, 2000). *Objectives* should be time bound and measurable. Examples of objectives include "improving performance by reducing waste by 5 percent on assembly line x," or "improving customer service by increasing customer satisfaction

as measured by weekly customer surveys." Measurable components in objectives are expressed by one or more of the following: quantity (*how much?*), quality (*how well?*), cost (*how much?*), time (*how often?*), and customer service (*for whom?*)

WLP effort objectives are expressed for the entire WLP department, function, or effort. WLP effort objectives should describe how WLP will contribute to improving the organization, performance, and individuals. Objectives are essentially accountability statements that set forth what results should be obtained by the department, function, or effort in a given time span.

Implementing Step 3

To implement this step, managers of WLP should take steps to make the vision and purpose of the WLP effort more concrete. One way to do that is to establish goals and, from those, specific and measurable time-bound objectives for achievement. The process is not done once and then forgotten. Instead, it is a continuing process of asking such questions as:

♦ Who are our customers and stakeholders, and what do they really need to improve their performance?

♦ What philosophy should govern procedures for serving our customers and stakeholders?

♦ When should customers be served? Should WLP strive to anticipate their needs, meet their needs as they surface, or meet needs after they are recognized?

♦ Where should needs be met? On the job? Near the job? Off the job? What combination is best?

♦ Why should the needs be met? What measurable outcomes can be forecast? How can costs and benefits of learning and nonlearning interventions be estimated?

♦ How should needs be met? What learning and nonlearning interventions should be the special forte of the WLP effort? How are referrals made to other sources of assistance when necessary?

Use Step 3 of the worksheet in figure 5.1 to answer these questions and clarify the goals and objectives necessary to realize the vision of the WLP effort and build enthusiasm for it.

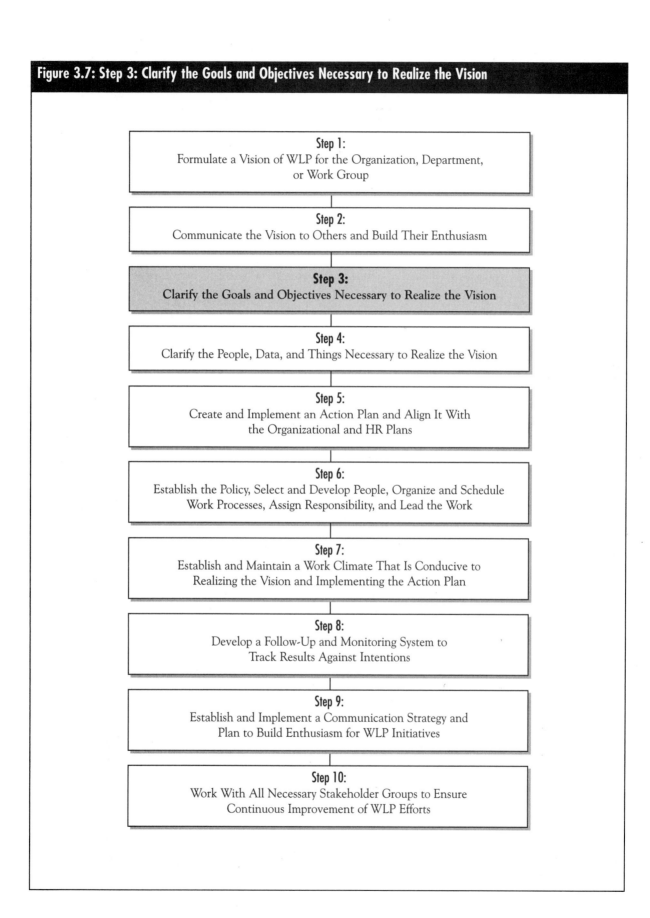

Figure 3.7: Step 3: Clarify the Goals and Objectives Necessary to Realize the Vision

Step 1:
Formulate a Vision of WLP for the Organization, Department, or Work Group

Step 2:
Communicate the Vision to Others and Build Their Enthusiasm

Step 3:
Clarify the Goals and Objectives Necessary to Realize the Vision

Step 4:
Clarify the People, Data, and Things Necessary to Realize the Vision

Step 5:
Create and Implement an Action Plan and Align It With the Organizational and HR Plans

Step 6:
Establish the Policy, Select and Develop People, Organize and Schedule Work Processes, Assign Responsibility, and Lead the Work

Step 7:
Establish and Maintain a Work Climate That Is Conducive to Realizing the Vision and Implementing the Action Plan

Step 8:
Develop a Follow-Up and Monitoring System to Track Results Against Intentions

Step 9:
Establish and Implement a Communication Strategy and Plan to Build Enthusiasm for WLP Initiatives

Step 10:
Work With All Necessary Stakeholder Groups to Ensure Continuous Improvement of WLP Efforts

Vignette: As a final item of business for the executive retreat for PQR Corporation, Miller gave senior managers the task of going a step beyond preparing a vision statement for the WLP department and considering the department's short-term (first-year) goals and objectives. He explained: "Your company has so many needs and so many competing interests that it is important to set priorities soon so that Edith Johnson has a chance of meeting them and is not overwhelmed. If you don't do that, nobody on earth could do all the things that you need or want in a short time. Therefore, we must make these goals realistic, achievable, and focused. We must then transform them into measurable objectives. Those, in turn, can be reviewed by a WLP Council that your group should later establish."

The senior managers divided up into small groups again to reflect on the following questions:

- Who are the specific customers inside PQR Corporation whose needs should be served first? (What group inside the company, if it is the focus of concentrated efforts, will most likely be the one that will yield the greatest payoffs? Why should it be the focus of initial attention?)

- What philosophy should govern the procedures used by the WLP department in serving those targeted customers?

- When should this first group of customers be served? Should WLP strive to anticipate their needs, meet their needs in real time as they surface, or meet needs after they are recognized?

- Where should needs be met? On the job? Near the job? Off the job? What combination is best?

- Why should the needs be met? What measurable outcomes can be forecast? How can costs and benefits of learning and nonlearning interventions be estimated?

- How should needs be met? What learning and nonlearning interventions should be the special forte of the WLP effort in the PQR Corporation?

Each group had an hour to discuss these questions. At the end of the time, a spokesperson

from each group presented a brief report. No agreement was quickly reached on what group should be the focus of initial attention or what kind of interventions should be the focus of the WLP department's attention. One group felt that supervisors should be the focus of initial attention, since few of them had received training and their impact on the hourly workforce was greatest. A second group felt that new hires at any or all levels should be the focus of initial attention, since their inability to learn the work quickly was a drain on productivity and morale and their ignorance was dangerous because it posed a safety hazard. A third group felt that production line employees should be the focus of greatest attention, since their numbers were largest and they had the greatest impact on getting the company's products manufactured and shipped.

It was eventually decided that Johnson should focus attention on newly hired assembly line workers during the first year. Other groups would be targeted later. Goals were expressed in terms of problems to be addressed. Objectives were kept relatively modest.

Step 4: Clarify the People, Data, and Things Necessary to Realize the Vision

Definition and Purpose of Step 4

This step has to do with clarifying what people, data (information), and things (objects, tools, and equipment) are needed to realize the vision of the WLP effort in the organization, department, or work group. Resources are necessary ingredients if a group is to realize a vision. This step clarifies what resources are necessary to transform the vision into reality. (See figure 3.8.)

Implementing Step 4

To implement this step, managers responsible for WLP should answer questions like these:

♦ How many and what kind of people are needed to achieve the goals and objectives of the WLP effort? How can they be justified on the basis of costs and benefits?

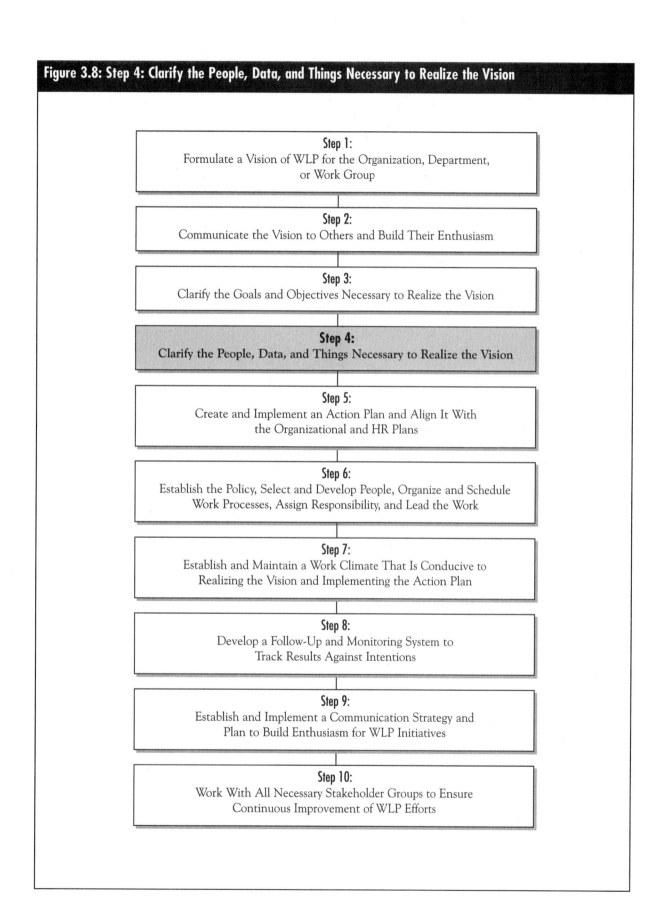

Figure 3.8: Step 4: Clarify the People, Data, and Things Necessary to Realize the Vision

Step 1:
Formulate a Vision of WLP for the Organization, Department, or Work Group

Step 2:
Communicate the Vision to Others and Build Their Enthusiasm

Step 3:
Clarify the Goals and Objectives Necessary to Realize the Vision

Step 4:
Clarify the People, Data, and Things Necessary to Realize the Vision

Step 5:
Create and Implement an Action Plan and Align It With the Organizational and HR Plans

Step 6:
Establish the Policy, Select and Develop People, Organize and Schedule Work Processes, Assign Responsibility, and Lead the Work

Step 7:
Establish and Maintain a Work Climate That Is Conducive to Realizing the Vision and Implementing the Action Plan

Step 8:
Develop a Follow-Up and Monitoring System to Track Results Against Intentions

Step 9:
Establish and Implement a Communication Strategy and Plan to Build Enthusiasm for WLP Initiatives

Step 10:
Work With All Necessary Stakeholder Groups to Ensure Continuous Improvement of WLP Efforts

- How much and what kind of data are needed to achieve the goals and objectives of the WLP effort?

- How much and what kind of things—including tools, equipment, and other objects, such as physical resources (buildings)—are needed to achieve the goals and objectives of the WLP effort?

By answering these questions, managers with responsibility for WLP can begin to determine how to realize the vision within the realistic constraints of resources available or obtainable. Use Step 4 of the worksheet in figure 5.1 to clarify the people, data, and things necessary to realize the vision.

Vignette: Following the executive retreat, the CEO and Edith Johnson met to talk about the next step for the organization, and Miller facilitated the meeting. Their focus was on the resources necessary to move forward now that the executive team was in basic agreement about the vision and purpose statements, goals, and objectives. The CEO suggested that the WLP manager consult with other managers and key stakeholders in the organization and then, together with the consultant, prepare a formal proposal for the senior executive group's review and approval.

The consultant asked the CEO to appoint a WLP Council that would include personnel from all areas of the organization: a member of the HR department, a senior executive, a middle manager, a technical worker (such as an engineer), a sales or marketing representative, a supervisor, and an hourly worker. (If the organization had been unionized, a union official would have been a member of the council as well.) The CEO asked Johnson to meet with the company's vice president of HR to brainstorm and nominate some staff members for the senior executive group to consider. Upon approval by that group, the WLP Council would be formally chartered as an advisory committee.

The council would have a few purposes:

- to broaden the ownership of WLP throughout the organization

- to establish recommendations for subsequent approval up the line

- to provide protection for the WLP manager.

Step 5: Create and Implement an Action Plan to Align With Organizational and HR Plans

Definition and Purpose of Step 5

Transforming a vision into a concrete action plan—or several of them—is often a necessary step in making a vision clear enough for people to implement it. (See figure 3.9.) As Ray (1997) points out, internal consultants must be effective in helping participants in an intervention to agree on a process, define the terms of the process, put a plan into action, and complete the action plan. And as Langdon (2000) has pointed out, ensuring alignment of interventions with organizational goals may be the key to success in the WLP field in the future.

Although many ways exist to align performance improvement interventions with organizational strategy, one particularly promising approach is to rely on the integrative power of competency modeling (Dubois and Rothwell, 2000; Horney and Koonce, 1996). Alignment occurs when everyday activities match the organization's mission, strategy, and values (Tosti and Jackson, 1994).

Implementing Step 5

To carry out this step, managers with WLP responsibilities must be able to establish a plan to realize the goals and objectives of the WLP effort. When the effort is limited to one intervention, the plan will resemble a project plan. But when the effort encompasses more than one intervention, such as all aspects of WLP for an organization, it resembles a strategic business plan.

Project plans focus attention on one intervention. For instance, if the organization will implement an initiative to improve customer service and will rely chiefly on a learning intervention, then the project plan will focus around the project elements. Often, managers of WLP will be tasked to prepare a proposal or a request for a proposal (RFP) to describe what is to be done. Typically, proposals take the form of answering such questions as these:

- What performance problem or business issue gives rise to the need for the intervention? What is the estimated cost of the problem, and on what basis was that estimated cost determined?

- What strategy for performance improvement is desirable to solve the problem or meet the

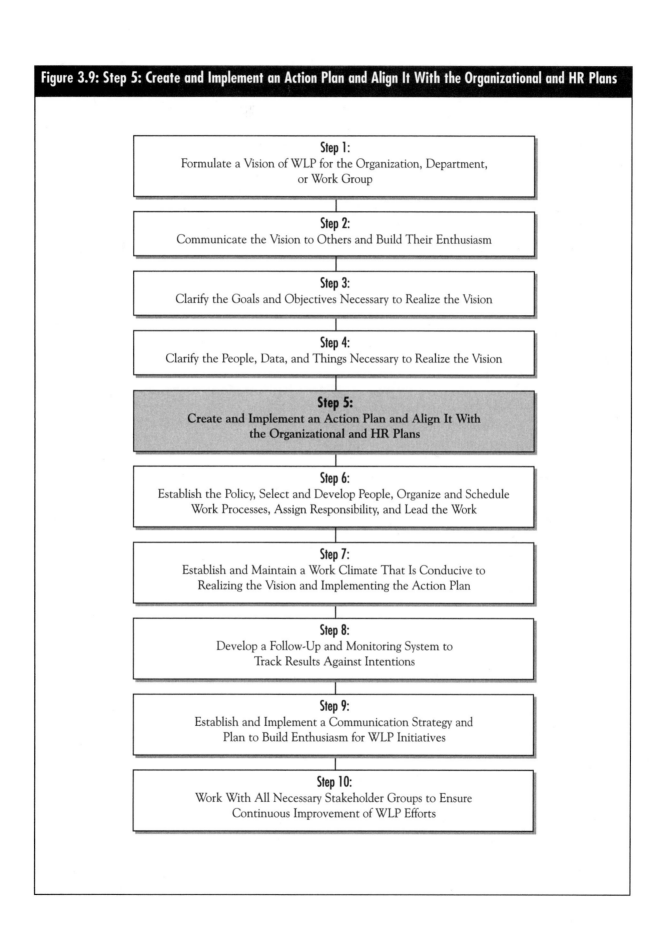

Step 1:
Formulate a Vision of WLP for the Organization, Department,
or Work Group

Step 2:
Communicate the Vision to Others and Build Their Enthusiasm

Step 3:
Clarify the Goals and Objectives Necessary to Realize the Vision

Step 4:
Clarify the People, Data, and Things Necessary to Realize the Vision

Step 5:
**Create and Implement an Action Plan and Align It With
the Organizational and HR Plans**

Step 6:
Establish the Policy, Select and Develop People, Organize and Schedule
Work Processes, Assign Responsibility, and Lead the Work

Step 7:
Establish and Maintain a Work Climate That Is Conducive to
Realizing the Vision and Implementing the Action Plan

Step 8:
Develop a Follow-Up and Monitoring System to
Track Results Against Intentions

Step 9:
Establish and Implement a Communication Strategy and
Plan to Build Enthusiasm for WLP Initiatives

Step 10:
Work With All Necessary Stakeholder Groups to Ensure
Continuous Improvement of WLP Efforts

business need? Why is that strategy preferable to obvious or cost-effective alternatives? What are the specific goals and objectives for the intervention?

♦ How will the intervention or project be aligned with organizational plans? With HR plans?

♦ How will the project be implemented? Through what step-by-step process will the project be undertaken? What outcomes or deliverables should be received from each step? How will the relative success of each step be measured? Who will be responsible for each step? What are the client's and consultant's responsibilities in each step?

♦ What is the timeline for the project? How long will the project take to implement, and what steps will be undertaken when? (This step is often expressed as a Gantt chart, with project steps compared to dates to show what steps might be undertaken simultaneously.)

♦ What is the budget for the project? What are the expected costs and benefits of the project?

♦ Who should participate in the project? What staff from inside and outside the organization will be necessary?

RFPs are written in a similar style except that they are written by a member of an organization to solicit help from a vendor or consultant. RFPs are meant to supply sufficient detail that a consultant can write a proposal based on the RFP alone. Most RFPs provide a detailed background statement about the organization and the performance problem, the organization's need for an intervention, one or more desirable solutions, and requests for a so-called technical proposal or technical work plan to meet identified objectives. RFPs may be much more detailed and may require consultants to supply evidence of errors-and-omission insurance coverage, assurances of who will work on a project, and other requirements.

Strategic plans are more comprehensive than project plans and typically describe the purpose of the WLP department, function, or effort, its goals and objectives, the external environment within which the WLP effort functions and the future threats and opportunities it poses, the present strengths and weaknesses of the WLP effort, a comparison of

future threats and opportunities and present strengths and weaknesses, a description of WLP strategies selected, a description of the implementation plan for the WLP effort or department, and a summary of how the WLP effort or department can be evaluated in comparison to its purpose, goals, and objectives.

Plans for WLP must also be aligned with the organization's objectives and the organization's HR plans. Organizational strategic objectives should indicate the long-term future competitive plans for an organization. WLP effort or department objectives can be double-checked against them (Sensenig, 1998).

HR plans should indicate how many and what kind of people will be needed by the organization over the long term to achieve strategic objectives (Rothwell and Kazanas, 1994b). They should also indicate how such HR initiatives as recruitment, selection, orientation, compensation, benefits, employee relations, human resource information systems (HRIS), discipline, and recruitment will be vertically aligned with the organization's strategic plan and how the initiatives will be horizontally aligned with each other (Rothwell, Prescott, and Taylor, 1998). WLP objectives should also be double-checked against HR plans and objectives to ensure horizontal alignment (Rothwell, Prescott, and Taylor, 1998).

Use Step 5 of the worksheet in figure 5.1 to answer the questions in this step, which guide you in thinking about how to create and implement an action plan to realize the vision and align the action plan with organizational plans and HR plans.

Vignette: External consultant Gregory Miller and Edith Johnson began writing a project proposal to meet the needs of production workers at PQR Corporation. Miller made his notes from interviews and focus groups that Johnson held. At Johnson's urging, Miller and she met with various managers and other key people at PQR Corporation to gather more specific information about their needs. By repeating the interviews at greater depth and concentrating on the needs of newly hired production workers, they would accomplish two objectives:

• Johnson would meet all the key stakeholders to get their individual perspectives.

- She would gather more information about the performance problems to be solved and the stakeholders' preferences and concerns about ways of meeting them.

Over a two-week time span, Johnson and Miller were able to meet with all the supervisors, managers, and executives associated with the production department. They were able to secure job descriptions of entry-level production workers, find out what training these workers received, and learn about the preferences of the vice president of manufacturing.

On the basis of that information and some external benchmarking, which Miller conducted, Johnson drafted a proposal for training entry-level production workers, and she prepared an oral presentation for delivery to the senior executive group at their next scheduled meeting.

While carrying out this task, Johnson and Miller also met with the vice president of human resources to identify people to serve on a company-wide WLP Council. When they made the initial selections, Miller suggested that they also identify the chief critic of WLP efforts and nominate that person for committee service. The vice president of HR placed the vice president of finance on the list to represent the strongest critic. He would also serve as spokesperson to the senior executive team about the WLP Council's operations.

Johnson and Miller presented the proposal to the senior executive team. After some modification, it was approved. The slate of names to serve on the companywide WLP Council was also approved.

Step 6: Establish the Policy, Select and Develop People, Organize and Schedule Work Processes, Assign Responsibility, and Lead the Work

Definition and Purpose of Step 6

This step has to do with making the action plan a reality by establishing policy, selecting the people, developing people, organizing and scheduling work processes, assigning responsibility to realize the vision, and leading the work of individuals and groups. These issues begin to transform long-term plans into intermediate-term plans to achieve results. (See figure 3.10.)

Establishing policy refers to clarifying what the organization wants and needs from WLP efforts. A policy is a description of what should be, and it is meant to coordinate decision making among many people (Rothwell and Kazanas, 1994a, 1994b; Rothwell and Sredl, 2000). Often, the process of writing a policy for WLP is useful because it encourages decision makers and stakeholders to think through what they want and need from WLP efforts and to reach some agreement on it. Key elements of a policy include explaining how WLP efforts align with organizational and HR plans, support achievement of individual career goals, and provide for meeting long-term and short-term performance improvement needs.

Selecting the people means clarifying how many and what kind of people are needed to activate the plan and thereby achieve the vision of the WLP effort. While it is possible to meet staffing needs through a combination of full-time staff, part-time staff, temporary staff, consultants, and outsourcing agents, managers of WLP must think through how many and what kind of people are needed to help achieve the requirements of the WLP effort (Rothwell, 1996). Since the competencies of those chosen for WLP positions affect the training they need and their capabilities, great care should be taken in choosing who will serve in WLP efforts. One powerful approach is to combine professional WLP knowledge and experience (obtained from outside the organization) with staff members who are knowledgeable about the company culture and work process (chosen from inside the organization).

Developing people means providing for the continuing training, education, and development of the WLP staff. Without that, WLP practitioners will feel like the proverbial shoemaker's children who go barefoot; they will be denied the very thing that they supply to others in the organization. Developmental efforts for WLP staff should help meet organizational and individual needs, as should WLP efforts for other workers in the organization. Of course, guidelines and recommendations for developing WLP staff members can be found in many places, such as *ASTD Models for Workplace Learning and Performance* (Rothwell, Sanders, and Soper, 1999), the *ASTD Reference Guide to Workplace Learning and Performance* (Rothwell and Sredl, 2000), and other job aids in this series.

Figure 3.10: Step 6: Establish the Policy, Select and Develop People, Organize and Schedule Work Processes, Assign Responsibility, and Lead the Work

Step 1:
Formulate a Vision of WLP for the Organization, Department, or Work Group

Step 2:
Communicate the Vision to Others and Build Their Enthusiasm

Step 3:
Clarify the Goals and Objectives Necessary to Realize the Vision

Step 4:
Clarify the People, Data, and Things Necessary to Realize the Vision

Step 5:
Create and Implement an Action Plan and Align It With the Organizational and HR Plans

Step 6:
Establish the Policy, Select and Develop People, Organize and Schedule Work Processes, Assign Responsibility, and Lead the Work

Step 7:
Establish and Maintain a Work Climate That Is Conducive to Realizing the Vision and Implementing the Action Plan

Step 8:
Develop a Follow-Up and Monitoring System to Track Results Against Intentions

Step 9:
Establish and Implement a Communication Strategy and Plan to Build Enthusiasm for WLP Initiatives

Step 10:
Work With All Necessary Stakeholder Groups to Ensure Continuous Improvement of WLP Efforts

Organizing and scheduling work processes means clarifying how the WLP effort will implement its plan and meet its goals and objectives on a continuing basis. Processes answer the questions: How is the work to be done, or how should the work be done? For instance, WLP practitioners may wish to create processes to govern how to respond to client requests, authorize projects, assign staff to projects, design and deliver interventions, and evaluate results. (In fact, each step in the HPI process model begs the question: How should each step in the model be carried out within the unique corporate culture of one organization?)

Assigning responsibility to realize the vision means clarifying who does what. It is management's responsibility to assign work responsibilities, so the manager of WLP should be accountable to ensure that necessary work has been assigned to people who are chosen and trained to carry it out. Responsibility can be assigned through such means as job descriptions, procedure manuals, policies, and responsibility charts that indicate who should do what tasks.

Leading the work of individuals and groups means that the manager with responsibility for WLP has an obligation to exert positive influence on others to communicate the mission or purpose of WLP in the organization, formulate and communicate policies stemming from that purpose, and energize people to achieve results and show performance improvements. Often, that means setting a personal example and being the first to leap into the work to get it done.

Implementing Step 6

To implement this step, managers responsible for WLP should pose such questions as these:

♦ What policies for WLP does the organization need?

♦ What policies for WLP may need to be changed as conditions affecting the organization change?

♦ What kind and how many people are needed now to carry out the purpose and achieve the goals and objectives of the WLP effort?

♦ What kind and how many people will be needed in the future to carry out the purpose and achieve the goals and objectives of the WLP effort?

♦ How should people bearing WLP responsibilities be developed now and in the future?

♦ How are work processes for WLP organized now? How should they be organized in the future?

♦ How are work processes for WLP scheduled now? How should they be scheduled in the future?

♦ How are work responsibilities for WLP assigned now? How should they be assigned in the future?

♦ How are WLP staff members being led now? How should they be led in the future in ways that will encourage them to achieve the desired work results?

Use Step 6 of the worksheet in figure 5.1 to answer these questions that guide you in thinking about how to establish an organization's WLP policy, select people for work in WLP, develop people for WLP work, organize and schedule work processes linked to WLP, assign responsibility to WLP staff to realize the vision, and lead the work of individuals and groups as they work toward WLP.

Vignette: After obtaining approval on the proposal for the training and subsequent socialization of entry-level assembly line workers at PQR Corporation, Edith Johnson organized the first meeting of the companywide WLP Council, and Gregory Miller served as facilitator.

The CEO opened the meeting, emphasizing the importance of the council, explaining that participants were chosen on the basis of their track records as exemplary performers, and describing their membership on the committee as an honor and privilege. The council members' role was to draft company WLP policy, present it for approval to senior managers, provide guidance on individual projects to the WLP manager, and chair ad hoc committees as needed to undertake specific performance improvement interventions.

The CEO turned the committee over to the company's vice president of finance, whom the senior management group chose to chair the committee. The VP of finance asked the consultant to make a brief presentation about possible next steps for the committee.

Miller presented a case study of another company that had faced the same challenge. He explained that that committee had focused its attention initially on five areas: drafting a formal charter to govern its operations, including the length of time served by members and how replacements would be chosen; drafting a formal policy and procedure to govern WLP efforts; creating a training plan by department, job level, and time in grade to govern off-the-job training requirements; improving on-the-job training practices in order to slash the unproductive breaking-in period of newcomers and increase worker retention; and selecting and implementing a record-keeping system that could be integrated with the company's payroll system to keep track of company training.

He said he had met with the company's WLP Council for a three-year time span. Although he was not advocating that PQR Corporation should follow in the footsteps of another company, he was giving that example so that council members would begin to see the need to develop a workable action plan to govern the long-term startup of the WLP department. He presented the committee members with a list of questions:

- What policy should govern the WLP Council at PQR Corporation?
- What policies for WLP does the organization need, and in what form should they be prepared?
- How could the company integrate its WLP efforts with strategic plans?

Committee members spent most of the first meeting getting acquainted and brainstorming on the next steps. By the end of the meeting, the vice president of finance summarized the results and requested that individuals volunteer to draft specific documents. Several people volunteered, and promised to return to the next meeting with draft documents.

Step 7: Establish and Maintain a Work Climate That Is Conducive to Realizing the Vision and Implementing the Action Plan

Definition and Purpose of Step 7

A work climate should encourage WLP practitioners to achieve results to the peak of their ability. Managers with WLP responsibilities should be concerned about performance management, the continuing process linked to building a high-performance workplace (Dubois and Rothwell, 1996a, 1996b). (See figure 3.11.)

Work climate refers to the psychological feel of the workplace. If you ask someone, "How do you feel about the place you work?" that person's answer will reflect what he or she perceives about the work climate. Climate should not be confused with *corporate culture*, which refers to the unspoken rules about how things are done and what is right and what is wrong in the workplace. Climate has more to do with how people feel about what they do, where they work, how their supervisors treat them, how psychologically secure they feel in the place they work, and what barriers get in the way of their achieving maximum results.

A manager with WLP responsibility has accountability for establishing and maintaining a work climate that is conducive to realizing the vision for WLP and implementing the action plan. If the manager does not do that, then he or she may find that WLP staff do not understand what the WLP department is trying to achieve, have no commitment to that purpose or those goals, and may eventually resign due to stress or poor job satisfaction. Ideally, the manager's job is to clarify for staff what results are sought and why they are sought, identify barriers or problems that get in the way of goal accomplishment, and help staff members knock down unnecessary barriers so that staff members are not frustrated by problems that they did not create.

Implementing Step 7

To implement this step, managers responsible for WLP should pose such questions as these:

- What is the current climate of the WLP department or project? What should be the climate in the opinion of WLP staff members?
- What barriers to performance or causes of dissatisfaction are evident among WLP staff? What causes them?
- How can the barriers to performance or causes of dissatisfaction be addressed?

Use Step 7 of the worksheet in figure 5.1 to answer these questions about how to establish and maintain a work climate that is conducive to realizing the vision of the WLP effort and implementing its action plan.

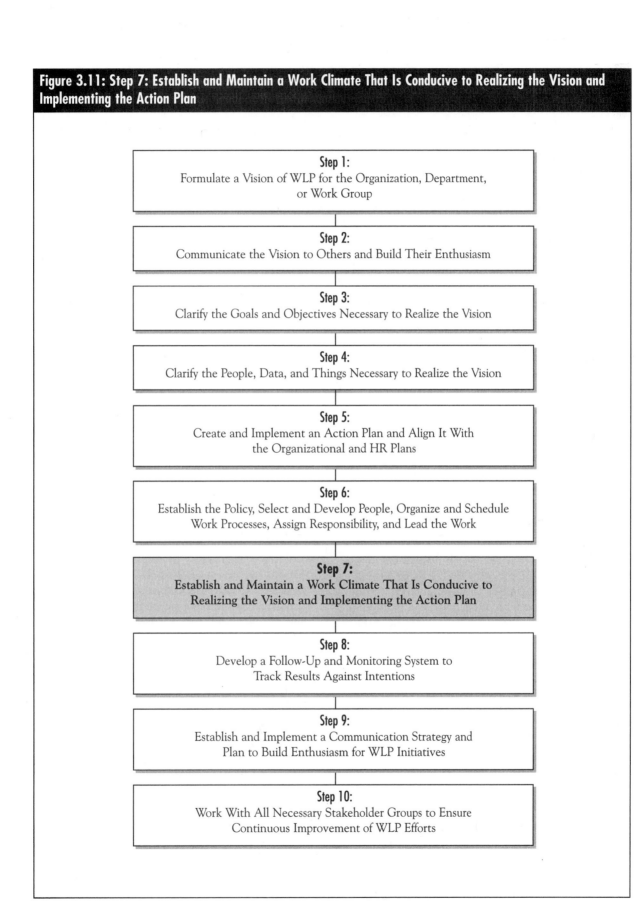

Step 1:
Formulate a Vision of WLP for the Organization, Department, or Work Group

Step 2:
Communicate the Vision to Others and Build Their Enthusiasm

Step 3:
Clarify the Goals and Objectives Necessary to Realize the Vision

Step 4:
Clarify the People, Data, and Things Necessary to Realize the Vision

Step 5:
Create and Implement an Action Plan and Align It With the Organizational and HR Plans

Step 6:
Establish the Policy, Select and Develop People, Organize and Schedule Work Processes, Assign Responsibility, and Lead the Work

Step 7:
Establish and Maintain a Work Climate That Is Conducive to Realizing the Vision and Implementing the Action Plan

Step 8:
Develop a Follow-Up and Monitoring System to Track Results Against Intentions

Step 9:
Establish and Implement a Communication Strategy and Plan to Build Enthusiasm for WLP Initiatives

Step 10:
Work With All Necessary Stakeholder Groups to Ensure Continuous Improvement of WLP Efforts

Vignette: Since Edith Johnson, the WLP manager, was hired by PQR Corporation to set up a WLP department from scratch, she did not think she needed to focus much attention on establishing a positive work climate for the department. As she joked with consultant Miller, "I am a one-person department, and the only boss I have to worry about is the CEO. I hope I am old enough to manage my own morale."

However, the consultant emphasized that it is important for a WLP department to set the example of a good working climate that will encourage peak performance. Although Johnson's is a one-person department now, it will soon grow. Through their discussions, she resolved to institute certain policies that would create a positive work climate. She would hold at least weekly staff meetings to discuss important issues and would implement an open-door policy so that every staff member would feel welcome to visit her at any time to discuss any problem.

Step 8: Develop a Follow-Up and Monitoring System to Track Results Against Intentions

Definition and Purpose of Step 8

It is not enough to devise and implement a plan. Some kind of follow-up and monitoring system is necessary to track results and feed them back to key stakeholders. Examples of such systems might include weekly activity or results reports, applications of online project management software so that everyone knows how all projects are proceeding and are planned, and calendars of events for facilities and for staff members. While this activity closely resembles the type of responsibility incumbent on the evaluator's and change leader's roles, it is nevertheless important for managers with WLP responsibilities to require that such a system be established and maintained. The operation of the system can eventually be turned over to others, but the manager has the responsibility to ensure that such a system is established and is continuously functioning. (See figure 3.12.)

Some managers with WLP responsibilities prefer to establish a balanced scorecard approach to evaluating and tracking results. Such an approach focuses evaluation on four areas: financial performance,

customer satisfaction, internal processes, and documented learning and growth (Kaplan and Norton, 1996). Effective WLP managers know intuitively what Lingle and Schiemann (1996) have found through research: Organizations, departments, or functions that are measurement managed tend to outperform less well-disciplined operations, perhaps because the goals for achievement are more explicit and clear.

Implementing Step 8

To implement this step, managers responsible for WLP should pose such questions as these to stakeholders and customers:

- What approach will work best in the organization to provide follow-up and monitoring to stakeholders that will compare results to intentions?
- Who needs information about the results of WLP, and what will they do with those results?
- How can all relevant stakeholder groups use such a system?

Use Step 8 of the worksheet in figure 5.1 to answer these questions and consider how to develop a follow-up and monitoring system to track results against intentions for WLP in the organization, department, or work group.

Vignette: At PQR Corporation, the consultant advised Edith Johnson to establish a tracking system to measure the results she gets. "The WLP manager has a responsibility to give his or her customers and stakeholders feedback on what returns they received for their investments of time, money, and effort," he said. He explained that different groups in the company will want different types of information, so Johnson must be sure to answer the questions for implementing the step so that she will understand what the stakeholders want to know. Senior executives might want to know what financial gains were realized from WLP efforts, for example. Operating middle managers might be far more interested in whether WLP efforts helped to solve business problems than whether they helped the organization gain money. Workers might care how WLP efforts help them get ahead and stay employed. In some organizations, it might be enough to provide the results of participant evaluations.

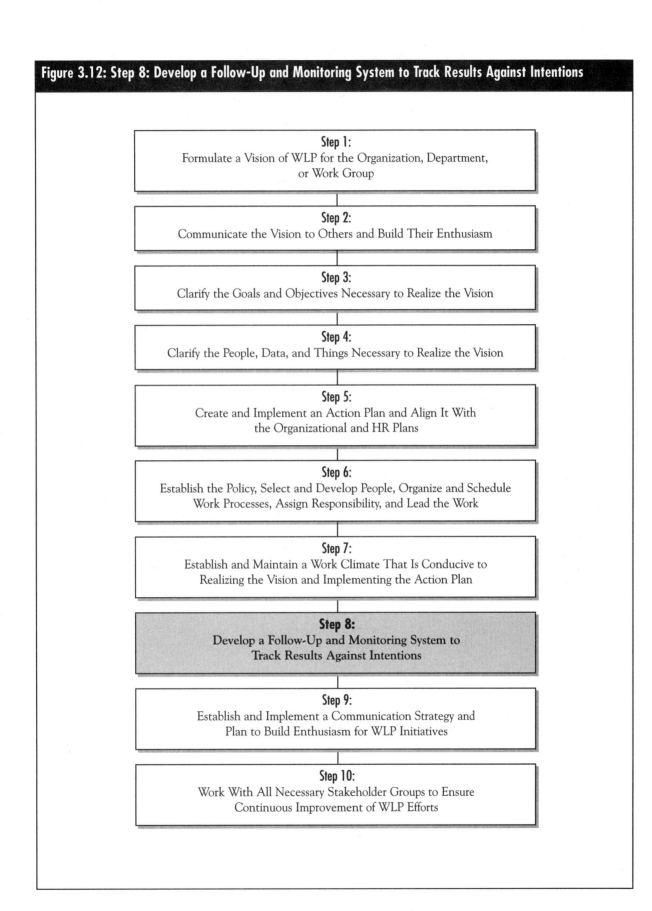

Step 1:
Formulate a Vision of WLP for the Organization, Department, or Work Group

Step 2:
Communicate the Vision to Others and Build Their Enthusiasm

Step 3:
Clarify the Goals and Objectives Necessary to Realize the Vision

Step 4:
Clarify the People, Data, and Things Necessary to Realize the Vision

Step 5:
Create and Implement an Action Plan and Align It With the Organizational and HR Plans

Step 6:
Establish the Policy, Select and Develop People, Organize and Schedule Work Processes, Assign Responsibility, and Lead the Work

Step 7:
Establish and Maintain a Work Climate That Is Conducive to Realizing the Vision and Implementing the Action Plan

Step 8:
Develop a Follow-Up and Monitoring System to Track Results Against Intentions

Step 9:
Establish and Implement a Communication Strategy and Plan to Build Enthusiasm for WLP Initiatives

Step 10:
Work With All Necessary Stakeholder Groups to Ensure Continuous Improvement of WLP Efforts

Step 9: Establish and Implement a Communication Strategy and Plan to Build Enthusiasm for WLP Initiatives

Definition and Purpose of Step 9

Stakeholders will not know how valuable WLP efforts have been to them and to the organization if no effort is made to let them know. It is important to establish and implement a communication strategy and plan that will build enthusiasm for WLP initiatives. Step 9 will achieve that. (See figure 3.13.)

A *communication strategy* is an integrated approach to communicating with key stakeholders in an organization. Just as an organizational strategy is how an organization competes, a communication strategy is how an organization, department, or work group communicates with others. It focuses attention on who should receive information, what kind of information those people should receive, when they want to receive that information, where they want to receive that information, why they are communicating, and how they will communicate.

Implementing Step 9

To implement this step, managers responsible for WLP should pose such questions as these:

♦ Who should receive information about WLP efforts?

♦ What kind of information should they receive?

♦ When should the WLP effort or department communicate with others?

♦ Where should the WLP effort or department communicate with others?

♦ Why should the WLP effort or department communicate?

♦ How should the WLP effort or department communicate with others?

Use Step 9 of the worksheet in figure 5.1 to ponder how to establish and implement a communication strategy and plan to build enthusiasm for WLP initiatives.

Vignette: Gregory Miller worked with Edith Johnson on developing a strategy and plan to build enthusiasm for WLP initiatives. They resolved that the plan should focus on how she would communicate

what she is doing to many people in the organization. It would tell how the WLP initiatives improve the company's performance, what its results are, and what future opportunities for improvement would open up for the company. Once a tracking and monitoring system was developed, she would need a communication strategy by which to present her results to a broader audience.

She and Miller decided to ask the WLP Council for advice and to regard the discussions with the council as part of the communication strategy. Some options they discussed proposing to the council were establishing a Website, having Johnson write regular columns for the company newsletter, and distributing action reports for regular distribution to the senior executives. Johnson's aim was to find a continuing, reliable way to reach the stakeholders. She used the questions in this section to guide her thinking before she met with the council and throughout the process of establishing and implementing the communication strategy.

Step 10: Work With All Necessary Stakeholder Groups to Ensure Continuous Improvement of WLP Efforts

Definition and Purpose of Step 10

The 10th and final step of the management process is that managers with WLP responsibilities should work with all necessary stakeholder groups to ensure continuous improvement of WLP efforts. (See figure 3.14.)

Implementing Step 10

To implement this step, managers responsible for WLP should pose questions like these to stakeholders and customers:

♦ Who should be included in continuous improvement efforts for WLP in the organization?

♦ What should be the focus of improvement for WLP?

♦ When or how often should improvement efforts be undertaken for WLP?

♦ Where (in what locations), if any, should continuous improvement efforts for WLP be focused?

♦ What results should be tracked and monitored from continuous improvement efforts for WLP?

Step 1:
Formulate a Vision of WLP for the Organization, Department, or Work Group

Step 2:
Communicate the Vision to Others and Build Their Enthusiasm

Step 3:
Clarify the Goals and Objectives Necessary to Realize the Vision

Step 4:
Clarify the People, Data, and Things Necessary to Realize the Vision

Step 5:
Create and Implement an Action Plan and Align It With the Organizational and HR Plans

Step 6:
Establish the Policy, Select and Develop People, Organize and Schedule Work Processes, Assign Responsibility, and Lead the Work

Step 7:
Establish and Maintain a Work Climate That Is Conducive to Realizing the Vision and Implementing the Action Plan

Step 8:
Develop a Follow-Up and Monitoring System to Track Results Against Intentions

Step 9:
Establish and Implement a Communication Strategy and Plan to Build Enthusiasm for WLP Initiatives

Step 10:
Work With All Necessary Stakeholder Groups to Ensure Continuous Improvement of WLP Efforts

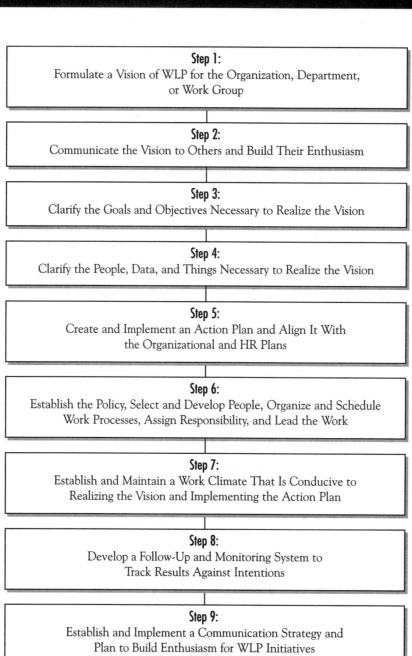

Step 1:
Formulate a Vision of WLP for the Organization, Department, or Work Group

Step 2:
Communicate the Vision to Others and Build Their Enthusiasm

Step 3:
Clarify the Goals and Objectives Necessary to Realize the Vision

Step 4:
Clarify the People, Data, and Things Necessary to Realize the Vision

Step 5:
Create and Implement an Action Plan and Align It With the Organizational and HR Plans

Step 6:
Establish the Policy, Select and Develop People, Organize and Schedule Work Processes, Assign Responsibility, and Lead the Work

Step 7:
Establish and Maintain a Work Climate That Is Conducive to Realizing the Vision and Implementing the Action Plan

Step 8:
Develop a Follow-Up and Monitoring System to Track Results Against Intentions

Step 9:
Establish and Implement a Communication Strategy and Plan to Build Enthusiasm for WLP Initiatives

Step 10:
Work With All Necessary Stakeholder Groups to Ensure Continuous Improvement of WLP Efforts

♦ How should continuous improvement efforts for WLP efforts be undertaken?

Use Step 10 of the worksheet in figure 5.1 to answer these questions on how to work with all necessary stakeholder groups to ensure continuous improvement of WLP efforts.

Vignette: Gregory Miller and Edith Johnson explored ways to ensure the continuous improvement of her department and performance interventions. The WLP Council would help to serve that purpose, but it would give only partial information. They decided that Johnson would have to establish a regular, annual review of the entire WLP function. Miller recommended that an outside consultant conduct a multirater 360 feedback assessment of the department, with a formal report that lists strengths, weaknesses, and specific recommendations for improvement. Johnson would present the report to the WLP Council.

Section Summary

This section describes how to enact the role of manager, the role that "plans, organizes, schedules, monitors, and leads the work of individuals and groups to attain desired results; facilitates the strategic plan; ensures that workplace learning and performance is aligned with organizational needs and plans; and ensures the accomplishment of the administrative requirements of the function" (Rothwell, Sanders, and Soper, 1999, p. 43). When WLP practitioners or others enact this role, they establish a foundation for WLP in an organizational setting. When carrying out this role, managers of WLP:

1. Formulate a vision of WLP for the organization, department, or work group.

2. Communicate the vision to others and build their enthusiasm.

3. Clarify the goals and objectives necessary to realize the vision.

4. Clarify the people, data, and things necessary to realize the vision.

5. Create and implement an action plan to realize the vision.

6. Establish the policy, select and develop people, organize and schedule work processes, assign responsibility, and lead the work.

7. Establish and maintain a work climate that is conducive to realizing the vision and implementing the action plan.

8. Develop a follow-up and monitoring system to track results against intentions.

9. Establish and implement a communication strategy and plan to build enthusiasm for WLP initiatives.

10. Work with all necessary stakeholder groups to ensure continuous improvement of WLP efforts.

The manager's role is logically related to the change leader's role, which is described in the next section.

SECTION 1   GETTING STARTED

SECTION 2   DEFINING THE ROLES

SECTION 3   ENACTING THE ROLE OF MANAGER

SECTION 4   ENACTING THE ROLE OF CHANGE LEADER

◆ Model of the Change Leadership Process

◆ Steps in the Change Leadership Process

— Step 1: Identify the Stakeholders Who Stand to Gain From the Benefits of an Intervention

— Step 2: Formulate a Strategy for Collecting the Results of the Intervention and Communicating Them to Key Stakeholders

— Step 3: Resolve Conflicts That Arise During Interventions

— Step 4: Communicate the Results to Excite Enthusiasm and Inspire Others About the Intervention

◆ Section Summary

SECTION 5   TOOLS FOR CONDUCTING MANAGEMENT AND CHANGE LEADERSHIP

SECTION 6   AFTERWORD

SECTION 7   BIBLIOGRAPHY

As defined in Section 2, the change leader "inspires the workforce to embrace the change, creates a direction for the change effort, helps the organization's workforce to adapt to the change, and ensures that interventions are continuously monitored and directed in ways that are consistent with stakeholders' desired results" (Rothwell, Sanders, and Soper, 1999, p. 43). It is the change leader's responsibility to excite interest and support around the interventions that are selected, designed and developed, and implemented to achieve results, solve performance problems, or seize improvement opportunities (Kotter, 1999; Russo, 1997).

In one sense, you might expect the change leader to serve as a sort of cheerleader for change, and that is an accurate perception. Change leaders use persuasive methods to involve, empower, interest, and build support during the implementation of the many interventions with which WLP practitioners may be involved (Whiteside, 1997). They also work to overcome the so-called set-up-to-fail syndrome that occurs when supervisors unwittingly set up their subordinates to fall short of expectations or company goals (Manzoni and Barsoux, 1998). As Dean Spitzer (1996) notes, effective performance improvement interventions are tied to organizational goals, begin at an auspicious time, enjoy management support, continuously solicit employee input, link interventions with other organizational initiatives, possess focused initial efforts, rely on a strong evaluation component, build in ways for regular communication, encourage ways to celebrate accomplishments, and are pursued persistently. The change leader helps to ensure that these characteristics of effective interventions occur on a continuing basis. Dess and Picken (2000) note that future leaders, such as those working tactically as change leaders on performance improvement interventions, must focus on the following:

♦ using strategic vision to motivate and inspire

♦ empowering employees at all levels

♦ accumulating and sharing internal knowledge

♦ gathering and integrating external information

♦ challenging the status quo

♦ enabling employees' creativity.

These same traits may also characterize future effective change leaders for WLP.

A change leadership process model can help WLP practitioners and other people carry out effective change leadership. As with other models of WLP roles, each step in the change leadership process model requires WLP practitioners (or others) to take action.

Model of the Change Leadership Process

Think of the change leadership process as a series of general steps as follows:

1. Identify the stakeholders who stand to gain from the benefits of an intervention.

2. Formulate a strategy for collecting the results of the intervention and communicating them to key stakeholders.

3. Resolve conflicts that arise during interventions.

4. Communicate the results to excite enthusiasm and inspire others about the intervention.

These steps are depicted in figure 4.1, and their relationship to the change leader's competencies are depicted in table 4.1. This section addresses these steps and provides guidance for applying them. As you think about change leadership, use figure 5.2, "Worksheet to Guide Change Leadership," on page 106 to help pose questions related to each step of the model.

While communication is an important process in all WLP roles, change leaders focus on the day-to-day processes of resolving conflicts, building interest, and showing the benefits of interventions. A key challenge change leaders face is how to unlock individual initiative during interventions (Frohman, 1997). Change leaders are acutely aware that organizations are communities, and change leaders work to promote eight key qualities that promote that workplace-as-community concept (Zemke, 1996):

♦ An alignment of values exists between management and all employee levels.

♦ The structure is employee based.

♦ Teamwork is encouraged.

♦ Open communication is more than lip service. It is practiced.

♦ Workers support each other.

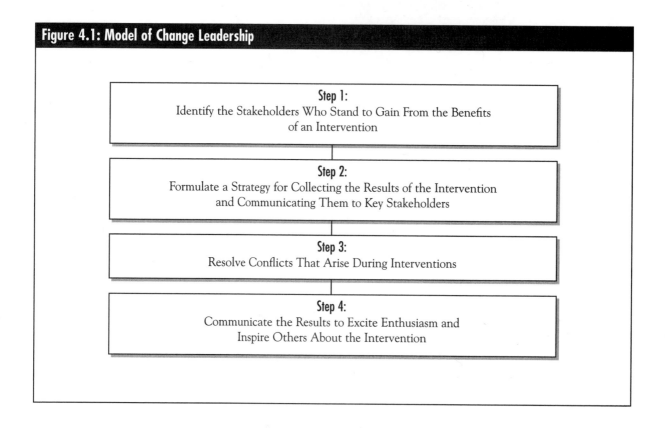

Figure 4.1: Model of Change Leadership

> **Step 1:**
> Identify the Stakeholders Who Stand to Gain From the Benefits of an Intervention

> **Step 2:**
> Formulate a Strategy for Collecting the Results of the Intervention and Communicating Them to Key Stakeholders

> **Step 3:**
> Resolve Conflicts That Arise During Interventions

> **Step 4:**
> Communicate the Results to Excite Enthusiasm and Inspire Others About the Intervention

Table 4.1: Relationship Between Change Leadership and the Competencies of the Change Leader*

Model of Change Leadership	Competencies of the Change Leader
Identify the Stakeholders Who Stand to Gain From the Benefits of an Intervention	◆ *Ability to see the big picture:* Identifying trends and patterns that are outside the normal paradigm of the organization. ◆ *Analytical thinking:* Clarifying complex issues by breaking them down into meaningful components and synthesizing related items. ◆ *Analyzing performance data:* Interpreting performance data and determining the effect of interventions on customers, suppliers, and employees. ◆ *Business knowledge:* Demonstrating awareness of business functions and how business decisions affect financial and nonfinancial work results. ◆ *Buy-in advocacy:* Building ownership and support for workplace initiatives. ◆ *Career development theory and application:* Understanding the theories, techniques, and appropriate applications of career development interventions used for performance improvement. ◆ *Consulting:* Understanding the results that stakeholders desire from a process and providing insight into how they can best use their resources to achieve goals. ◆ *Diversity awareness:* Assessing the impact and appropriateness of interventions on individuals, groups, and organizations. ◆ *Industry awareness:* Understanding the current and future climate of the organization's industry and formulating strategies that respond to that climate. ◆ *Interpersonal relationship building:* Effectively interacting with others in order to produce meaningful outcomes.

*Some competencies are used in more than one step of the model.

Model of Change Leadership	Competencies of the Change Leader

Identify the Stakeholders Who Stand to Gain From the Benefits of an Intervention
(continued)

♦ *Knowledge management:* Developing and implementing systems for creating, managing, and distributing knowledge.
♦ *Model building:* Conceptualizing and developing theoretical and practical frameworks that describe complex ideas.
♦ *Performance theory:* Recognizing the implications, outcomes, and consequences of performance interventions to distinguish between activities and results.
♦ *Quality implications:* Identifying the relationships and implications of quality programs and performance.
♦ *Social awareness:* Seeing organizations as dynamic political, economic, and social systems.
♦ *Standards identification:* Determining what constitutes success for individuals, organizations, and processes.
♦ *Work environment analysis:* Examining the work environment for issues or characteristics that affect human performance; understanding characteristics of a high-performance workplace.

Formulate a Strategy for Collecting the Results of the Intervention and Communicating Them to Key Stakeholders

♦ *Ability to see the big picture:* Identifying trends and patterns that are outside the normal paradigm of the organization.
♦ *Analytical thinking:* Clarifying complex issues by breaking them down into meaningful components and synthesizing related items.
♦ *Analyzing performance data:* Interpreting performance data and determining the effect of interventions on customers, suppliers, and employees.
♦ *Business knowledge:* Demonstrating awareness of business functions and how business decisions affect financial and nonfinancial work results.
♦ *Buy-in advocacy:* Building ownership and support for workplace initiatives.
♦ *Communication:* Applying effective verbal, nonverbal, and written communication methods to achieve desired results.
♦ *Communication networks:* Understanding the various methods through which communication is achieved.
♦ *Consulting:* Understanding the results that stakeholders desire from a process and providing insight into how they can best use their resources to achieve goals.
♦ *Diversity awareness:* Assessing the impact and appropriateness of interventions on individuals, groups, and organizations.
♦ *Evaluation of results against organizational goals:* Assessing how well workplace performance, learning strategies, and results match organizational goals and strategic intent.
♦ *Group dynamics:* Assessing how groups of people function and evolve as they seek to meet the needs of their members and of the organization.
♦ *Identification of critical business issues:* Determining key business issues and forces for change and applying that knowledge to performance improvement strategies.
♦ *Interpersonal relationship building:* Effectively interacting with others in order to produce meaningful outcomes.
♦ *Model building:* Conceptualizing and developing theoretical and practical frameworks that describe complex ideas.

(continued on next page)

Table 4.1: Relationship Between Change Leadership and the Competencies of the Change Leader (continued)

Model of Change Leadership	Competencies of the Change Leader
Formulate a Strategy for Collecting the Results of the Intervention and Communicating Them to Key Stakeholders (*continued*)	◆ *Performance theory:* Recognizing the implications, outcomes, and consequences of performance interventions to distinguish between activities and results. ◆ *Process consultation:* Using a monitoring and feedback method to continually improve the productivity of work groups. ◆ *Project management:* Planning, organizing, and monitoring work. ◆ *Quality implications:* Identifying the relationships and implications of quality programs and performance. ◆ *Social awareness:* Seeing organizations as dynamic political, economic, and social systems. ◆ *Standards identification:* Determining what constitutes success for individuals, organizations, and processes. ◆ *Systems thinking:* Recognizing the interrelationship among events by determining the driving forces that connect seemingly isolated incidents within the organization; taking a holistic view of performance problems in order to find root causes. ◆ *Visioning:* Seeing the possibilities of what can be and inspiring a shared sense of purpose within the organization. ◆ *Work environment analysis:* Examining the work environment for issues or characteristics that affect human performance; understanding characteristics of a high-performance workplace. ◆ *Workplace performance, learning strategies, and intervention evaluation:* Continually evaluating and improving interventions before and during implementation.
Resolve Conflicts That Arise During Interventions	◆ *Ability to see the big picture:* Identifying trends and patterns that are outside the normal paradigm of the organization. ◆ *Analytical thinking:* Clarifying complex issues by breaking them down into meaningful components and synthesizing related items. ◆ *Analyzing performance data:* Interpreting performance data and determining the effect of interventions on customers, suppliers, and employees. ◆ *Business knowledge:* Demonstrating awareness of business functions and how business decisions affect financial and nonfinancial work results. ◆ *Buy-in advocacy:* Building ownership and support for workplace initiatives. ◆ *Career development theory and application:* Understanding the theories, techniques, and appropriate applications of career development interventions used for performance improvement. ◆ *Communication:* Applying effective verbal, nonverbal, and written communication methods to achieve desired results. ◆ *Communication networks:* Understanding the various methods through which communication is achieved. ◆ *Consulting:* Understanding the results that stakeholders desire from a process and providing insight into how they can best use their resources to achieve goals. ◆ *Coping skills:* Dealing with ambiguity and stress resulting from conflicting information and goals; helping others deal with ambiguity and stress. ◆ *Diversity awareness:* Assessing the impact and appropriateness of interventions on individuals, groups, and organizations. ◆ *Ethics modeling:* Modeling exemplary ethical behavior and understanding the implications of this responsibility.

Model of Change Leadership	Competencies of the Change Leader

Resolve Conflicts That Arise During Interventions
(continued)

♦ *Evaluation of results against organizational goals:* Assessing how well workplace performance, learning strategies, and results match organizational goals and strategic intent.

♦ *Facilitation:* Helping others to discover new insights.

♦ *Feedback:* Providing performance information to the appropriate people.

♦ *Group dynamics:* Assessing how groups of people function and evolve as they seek to meet the needs of their members and of the organization.

♦ *Identification of critical business issues:* Determining key business issues and forces for change and applying that knowledge to performance improvement strategies.

♦ *Industry awareness:* Understanding the current and future climate of the organization's industry and formulating strategies that respond to that climate.

♦ *Interpersonal relationship building:* Effectively interacting with others in order to produce meaningful outcomes.

♦ *Intervention monitoring:* Tracking and coordinating interventions to assure consistency in implementation and alignment with organizational strategies.

♦ *Knowledge capital:* Measuring knowledge capital and determining its value to the organization.

♦ *Knowledge management:* Developing and implementing systems for creating, managing, and distributing knowledge.

♦ *Leadership:* Leading, influencing, and coaching others to help them achieve desired results.

♦ *Model building:* Conceptualizing and developing theoretical and practical frameworks that describe complex ideas.

♦ *Organization development theory and application:* Understanding the theories, techniques, and appropriate applications of organization development interventions as they are used for performance improvement.

♦ *Outsourcing management:* Ability to identify and select specialized resources outside of the organization; identifying, selecting, and managing technical specifications for these specialized resources.

♦ *Performance theory:* Recognizing the implications, outcomes, and consequences of performance interventions to distinguish between activities and results.

♦ *Process consultation:* Using a monitoring and feedback method to continually improve the productivity of work groups.

♦ *Project management:* Planning, organizing, and monitoring work.

♦ *Quality implications:* Identifying the relationships and implications of quality programs and performance.

♦ *Reward system theory and application:* Understanding the theories, techniques, and appropriate applications of reward system interventions used for performance improvement.

♦ *Social awareness:* Seeing organizations as dynamic political, economic, and social systems.

♦ *Standards identification:* Determining what constitutes success for individuals, organizations, and processes.

♦ *Visioning:* Seeing the possibilities of what can be and inspiring a shared sense of purpose within the organization.

(continued on next page)

Model of Change Leadership	Competencies of the Change Leader
Resolve Conflicts That Arise During Interventions *(continued)*	♦ *Work environment analysis:* Examining the work environment for issues or characteristics that affect human performance; understanding characteristics of a high-performance workplace. ♦ *Workplace performance, learning strategies, and intervention evaluation:* Continually evaluating and improving interventions before and during implementation.
Communicate the Results to Excite Enthusiasm and Inspire Others About the Intervention	♦ *Ability to see the big picture:* Identifying trends and patterns that are outside the normal paradigm of the organization. ♦ *Adult learning:* Understanding how adults learn and how they use knowledge, skills, and attitudes. ♦ *Analytical thinking:* Clarifying complex issues by breaking them down into meaningful components and synthesizing related items. ♦ *Analyzing performance data:* Interpreting performance data and determining the effect of interventions on customers, suppliers, and employees. ♦ *Business knowledge:* Demonstrating awareness of business functions and how business decisions affect financial and nonfinancial work results. ♦ *Buy-in advocacy:* Building ownership and support for workplace initiatives. ♦ *Career development theory and application:* Understanding the theories, techniques, and appropriate applications of career development interventions used for performance improvement. ♦ *Communication:* Applying effective verbal, nonverbal, and written communication methods to achieve desired results. ♦ *Communication networks:* Understanding the various methods through which communication is achieved. ♦ *Computer-mediated communication:* Understanding the implication of current and evolving computer-based electronic communication. ♦ *Consulting:* Understanding the results that stakeholders desire from a process and providing insight into how they can best use their resources to achieve goals. ♦ *Coping skills:* Dealing with ambiguity and stress resulting from conflicting information and goals; helping others deal with ambiguity and stress. ♦ *Diversity awareness:* Assessing the impact and appropriateness of interventions on individuals, groups, and organizations. ♦ *Evaluation of results against organizational goals:* Assessing how well workplace performance, learning strategies, and results match organizational goals and strategic intent. ♦ *Facilitation:* Helping others to discover new insights. ♦ *Feedback:* Providing performance information to the appropriate people. ♦ *Group dynamics:* Assessing how groups of people function and evolve as they seek to meet the needs of their members and of the organization. ♦ *Identification of critical business issues:* Determining key business issues and forces for change and applying that knowledge to performance improvement strategies. ♦ *Industry awareness:* Understanding the current and future climate of the organization's industry and formulating strategies that respond to that climate.

Model of Change Leadership	Competencies of the Change Leader
Communicate the Results to Excite Enthusiasm and Inspire Others About the Intervention (*continued*)	♦ *Interpersonal relationship building:* Effectively interacting with others in order to produce meaningful outcomes. ♦ *Intervention monitoring:* Tracking and coordinating interventions to assure consistency in implementation and alignment with organizational strategies. ♦ *Knowledge capital:* Measuring knowledge capital and determining its value to the organization. ♦ *Leadership:* Leading, influencing, and coaching others to help them achieve desired results. ♦ *Model building:* Conceptualizing and developing theoretical and practical frameworks that describe complex ideas. ♦ *Organization development theory and application:* Understanding the theories, techniques, and appropriate applications of organization development interventions as they are used for performance improvement. ♦ *Outsourcing management:* Ability to identify and select specialized resources outside of the organization; identifying, selecting, and managing technical specifications for these specialized resources. ♦ *Performance theory:* Recognizing the implications, outcomes, and consequences of performance interventions to distinguish between activities and results. ♦ *Process consultation:* Using a monitoring and feedback method to continually improve the productivity of work groups. ♦ *Project management:* Planning, organizing, and monitoring work. ♦ *Quality implications:* Identifying the relationships and implications of quality programs and performance. ♦ *Reward system theory and application:* Understanding the theories, techniques, and appropriate applications of reward system interventions used for performance improvement. ♦ *Social awareness:* Seeing organizations as dynamic political, economic, and social systems. ♦ *Standards identification:* Determining what constitutes success for individuals, organizations, and processes. ♦ *Systems thinking:* Recognizing the interrelationship among events by determining the driving forces that connect seemingly isolated incidents within the organization; taking a holistic view of performance problems in order to find root causes. ♦ *Technological literacy:* Understanding and appropriately applying existing, new, or emerging technology. ♦ *Visioning:* Seeing the possibilities of what can be and inspiring a shared sense of purpose within the organization. ♦ *Work environment analysis:* Examining the work environment for issues or characteristics that affect human performance; understanding characteristics of a high-performance workplace. ♦ *Workplace performance, learning strategies, and intervention evaluation:* Continually evaluating and improving interventions before and during implementation.

- Both an implicit and explicit respect for individuality is evident.

- The organization has permeable boundaries that do not prompt turf battles.

- Efforts are made to encourage periodic group renewal.

Steps in the Change Leadership Process

Each step of the change leadership process follows a similar format. The definition and purpose of the step appears first, notes about implementing or carrying out the steps follow, and then there is an example of the step to illustrate what it means in practice.

Step 1: Identify the Stakeholders Who Stand to Gain From the Benefits of an Intervention

Definition and Purpose of Step 1

Good change leaders, like good WLP managers and good evaluators, will usually begin by determining who is most interested in finding out about the results of an intervention. That is the process of identifying the stakeholders. (See figure 4.2.) After all, who is interested often influences such things as what they want to know, why they want to know it, and what actions they can and will take. Sherriton and Stern (1997) have pointed out that HR plays a part in any change effort by the following: assessing needs, securing and maintaining executive direction, building the necessary infrastructure to support the change, creating sufficient organization to help follow through on the change, offering training to teach people what they need to know and do to support change, and ensuring that results are tracked against intentions. The same basic approach may be applied for any intervention, and WLP has the same basic important role to play in it.

Implementing Step 1

Begin the change leadership process by posing the following questions to stakeholders:

- Who are the stakeholders who want or need information about the implementation or the progress of the intervention on a frequent basis?

- What kind of information do the stakeholders prefer to receive?

- How do the stakeholders prefer to receive information?

- How often do the stakeholders prefer to receive information?

Use Step 1 of the worksheet in figure 5.2 to address these questions to identify the stakeholders who stand to benefit from an intervention.

Vignette: Edith Johnson, PQR Corporation's WLP manager, and Gregory Miller, the consultant, addressed the critical importance of identifying the stakeholders and formulating ways to communicate with them. These activities are crucial to the success of an intervention geared to improving the training and socialization of entry-level assembly line workers. The consultant explained that a performance improvement intervention is a change effort, affecting many people. Those people must first be identified and then they will want someone to talk to, and the WLP manager is the obvious person. If she is not accessible, the complaints will end up destroying the effort because nobody is addressing them and facilitating real-time problem solving.

Miller made an analogy to the 1990 presidential campaign. "The winning Clinton campaign had a poster that was meant to focus the thinking of campaign workers and energize their efforts. It said something like 'It's the economy, stupid.' My advice to you in managing a performance improvement intervention is perhaps best summarized as 'It's discovering the stakeholders and communicating with them, stupid.' You must find a way to communicate all the time, and with as many stakeholders as possible, during an intervention." Some effective communication methods include regular briefing sessions, online bulletin boards on the company intranet, tangible bulletin boards in front of the employee cafeterias at all company locations, and regular coverage of the effort in the company newsletter."

The consultant reminded Johnson to think about the preceding key questions and find answers to them.

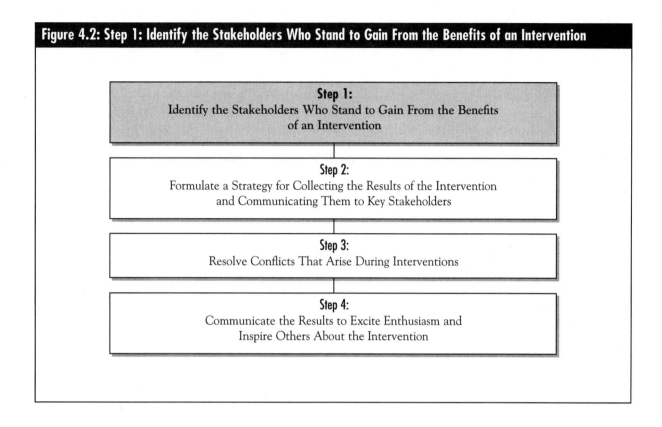

Figure 4.2: Step 1: Identify the Stakeholders Who Stand to Gain From the Benefits of an Intervention

Step 1:
Identify the Stakeholders Who Stand to Gain From the Benefits of an Intervention

Step 2:
Formulate a Strategy for Collecting the Results of the Intervention and Communicating Them to Key Stakeholders

Step 3:
Resolve Conflicts That Arise During Interventions

Step 4:
Communicate the Results to Excite Enthusiasm and Inspire Others About the Intervention

Step 2: Formulate a Strategy for Collecting the Results of the Intervention and Communicating Them to Key Stakeholders

Definition and Purpose of Step 2

A strategy must be in place by which to collect the results from the intervention, on a continuing basis, and communicate them to key stakeholders. (See figure 4.3.) Unlike the role of WLP managers, who also bear communication responsibilities, change leaders function at a tactical level rather than a strategic level. They provide personal contact on a daily basis with the client and change participants involved in an intervention. The importance of such high-touch involvement should not be minimized. The reason is simple: People want to be involved in decisions affecting them, and personal contact gives them a chance to offer their ideas, complain about what is not working so well, offer suggestions for improvement, and (in short) come to own the change. Without that, people feel alienated and feel that nobody cares about their opinions. External

consultants sometimes call this *face time* with the client, and that is exactly what is needed to keep an intervention on the front burner and focused. Indeed, many failures in change efforts stem from the lack of a change leader to help with daily, continuing follow-up and follow-through (Markus and Benjamin, 1997).

Implementing Step 2

Implementation requires an answer to the question, What strategy will be most effective for communicating to stakeholders, on a continuing basis, about the intervention?

A study of highly successful organizations, carried out by Coopers and Lybrand and Opinion Research Corporation International, indicated that five factors are key success drivers in any change effort:

♦ strong leadership

♦ effective communication

♦ tight alignment of people and organizational goals

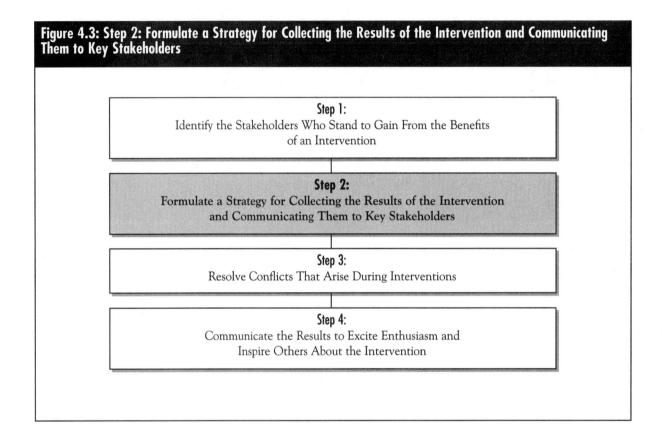

Figure 4.3: Step 2: Formulate a Strategy for Collecting the Results of the Intervention and Communicating Them to Key Stakeholders

Step 1:
Identify the Stakeholders Who Stand to Gain From the Benefits of an Intervention

Step 2:
Formulate a Strategy for Collecting the Results of the Intervention and Communicating Them to Key Stakeholders

Step 3:
Resolve Conflicts That Arise During Interventions

Step 4:
Communicate the Results to Excite Enthusiasm and Inspire Others About the Intervention

♦ adequate training and funding

♦ a clear definition of the compelling reasons for the change (Smith, 1998).

Clearly, communicating—which is also one of the factors—affects at least factors one and five of these success drivers. It is, after all, through communication that leaders exert influence over others, and it is through communicating that leaders make a compelling case for change.

Use Step 2 of the worksheet in figure 5.2 to answer this question and to formulate a strategy for collecting the results of the intervention and communicating them to key stakeholders.

Vignette: Gregory Miller, the consultant, emphasized to Edith Johnson, the WLP manager, the need for devising a strategy for communicating to stakeholders involved in a performance improvement intervention. "You need to let people know, or else find a way to let them inform each other, about how much progress is being made, any

roadblocks that appear along the way, and what issues should be the focus of attention. Remember that such communication is essential to success in implementing the intervention." This strategy differs from the one in which the WLP manager communicates about the department's efforts because the focus here is specifically on just one intervention, whereas the department may actually be involved in many such interventions. They concluded that the key question to answer is, What strategy will be most effective for collecting the results from the intervention and communicating, on a continuing basis, about the intervention to stakeholders? She decided to answer this question by asking the stakeholders for their opinions. Johnson posed the questions to her immediate supervisor and, with permission, in focus groups to other representatives of the organization. Because she had to work quickly, she supplemented this effort by sending emails for guidance to key line managers in the organization to give them a chance to offer suggestions about the strategy.

Step 3: Resolve Conflicts That Arise During Interventions

Definition and Purpose of Step 3

No intervention can be successfully implemented without conflict. There are two kinds of conflict: *Destructive conflict* focuses on the negative and is not helpful to improvement efforts; *constructive conflict* focuses on the positive and is inherently uplifting and geared toward improvements. Both destructive and constructive conflict occur during the course of an intervention's implementation. It is important in change leadership to know how to resolve such conflicts—or how to keep them from destroying an intervention. (See figure 4.4.) Four particular areas to watch during any change effort include the HR resource frame (which focuses on needs and skills); the structural frame (alignment and clarity); the political frame (conflict and arenas); and the symbolic frame (meaning and purpose) (Bolman and Deal, 1999). Resolving conflicts, of course, has to do with managing the political frame on a daily basis as it affects the implementation of an intervention.

Implementing Step 3

Resolve conflicts that arise during interventions by addressing such questions as these:

♦ What conflicts are likely to arise before an intervention?

♦ What conflicts are arising during the implementing of an intervention?

♦ What is the nature of the conflict? From what cause or causes does it stem?

♦ How many and what kinds of people are involved in, or are likely to be involved in, the conflict?

♦ How destructive is the conflict? How constructive?

♦ What strategies can be used by the change leader to focus attention on issues and goals and away from personalities?

♦ What strategies are most effective in resolving conflict? How can stakeholders be trained on conflict resolution techniques so that they are equipped to diagnose and resolve their own conflicts?

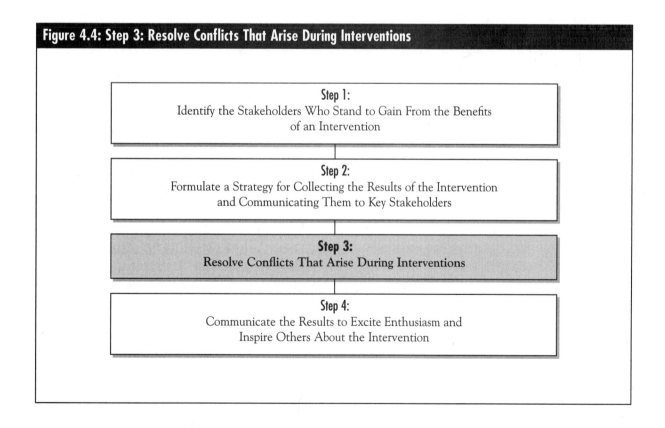

Figure 4.4: Step 3: Resolve Conflicts That Arise During Interventions

Step 1:
Identify the Stakeholders Who Stand to Gain From the Benefits of an Intervention

Step 2:
Formulate a Strategy for Collecting the Results of the Intervention and Communicating Them to Key Stakeholders

Step 3:
Resolve Conflicts That Arise During Interventions

Step 4:
Communicate the Results to Excite Enthusiasm and Inspire Others About the Intervention

Much has been written about conflict management and conflict resolution (Irvine, 1998; Klunk, 1997; Tamir, 1999). But most conflict resolution models stress the following: identifying the issues, identifying the sources of conflict, communicating openly, and focusing on problem solving rather than placing blame or attacking personalities.

Use Step 3 of the worksheet in figure 5.2 to pose the preceding questions to resolve conflicts that arise during interventions.

Vignette: Conflicts are likely to arise during any performance improvement intervention. The consultant Gregory Miller advised Edith Johnson to be prepared for them and resolve them early. Miller said, "When there's a conflict, you may need to search for the right language to use to help resolve it. Sometimes the parties to a conflict can provide you with that language. You can ask them what areas they find important and what areas they believe other groups find important. Their replies reveal a lot about how the parties view each other and guide you to the language to use in settling the differences. As an alternative, you might sit in on meetings and find out what people get excited about. There is almost always something that excites them."

Miller also recommended that Johnson provide key stakeholders with training on conflict resolution strategies early in the performance improvement intervention. One good approach is a model in which participants will learn to diagnose the causes of the conflict themselves and find solutions themselves. This technique is the best way to avoid the breakdown that can occur when parties to a conflict adopt the view that if others don't agree with them, there must be something wrong with them. Johnson agreed that it would be better to mediate by teaching people how to recognize a conflict, diagnose its causes, and reach strategies for moving forward in a positive way to achieve mutual goals.

Step 4: Communicate the Results to Excite Enthusiasm and Inspire Others About the Intervention

Definition and Purpose of Step 4

The fourth and final step of the change leadership process is to communicate the results of interventions to excite enthusiasm and inspire others. (See figure 4.5.) This step overlaps with that of the evaluator, since the evaluator's role involves making clear what results were gained from an intervention (Rothwell, 2000). A key difference between the role of evaluator and change leader is that the change leader communicates intervention results to build or sustain a momentum for change and to encourage and motivate stakeholders, whereas the evaluator's role is to assess the impact of interventions and follow up on "changes made, actions taken, and results achieved in order to provide participants and stakeholders with information about the effectiveness of intervention implementation" (Rothwell, Sanders, and Soper, 1999, p. xvii). More than 1,000 ways exist to inspire people during change (Rye, 1998).

Implementing Step 4

As you begin to communicate the results of interventions to excite enthusiasm and inspire others about it, address such questions as these:

♦ What are the key values of stakeholders?

♦ What results are different groups of stakeholders interested in, and why are they interested?

♦ How can positive results of interventions be communicated in a way that will be most encouraging and motivating to stakeholders?

♦ How can negative results of interventions be used to spur improvement efforts and avoid disappointment that is so keen that it demotivates improvement efforts?

Use Step 4 of the worksheet in figure 5.2 to address these questions about communicating the results of interventions to excite enthusiasm and inspire others about the intervention.

Vignette: Gregory Miller and Edith Johnson discussed the importance of communicating the results. "Act on the communication strategy you established," Miller said. They decided that Johnson will periodically find a way to celebrate successes and focus on problem solving rather than grieving about failures. She will remain focused on spreading the word about how a performance improvement intervention has mattered. Miller also advised her to get testimonials about the benefits of the intervention as they are

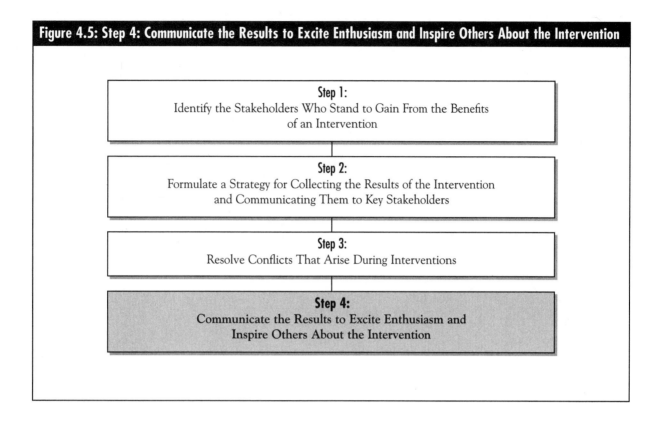

Figure 4.5: Step 4: Communicate the Results to Excite Enthusiasm and Inspire Others About the Intervention

> **Step 1:**
> Identify the Stakeholders Who Stand to Gain From the Benefits of an Intervention

> **Step 2:**
> Formulate a Strategy for Collecting the Results of the Intervention and Communicating Them to Key Stakeholders

> **Step 3:**
> Resolve Conflicts That Arise During Interventions

> **Step 4:**
> Communicate the Results to Excite Enthusiasm and Inspire Others About the Intervention

being realized and let other people hear those. "That is really one of the most effective strategies to use," Miller said.

Section Summary

This section described how to enact the role of change leader, defined as the role that "inspires the workforce to embrace the change, creates a direction for the change effort, helps the organization's workforce to adapt to the change, and ensures that interventions are continuously monitored and directed in ways that are consistent with stakeholders' desired results" (Rothwell, Sanders, and Soper, 1999,

p. 43). Key steps in carrying out change leadership include:

1. Identify the stakeholders who stand to gain from the benefits of an intervention.

2. Formulate a strategy for collecting the results of the intervention and communicating them to key stakeholders.

3. Resolve conflicts that arise during interventions.

4. Communicate the results to excite enthusiasm and inspire others about the intervention.

SECTION 1   GETTING STARTED

SECTION 2   DEFINING THE ROLES

SECTION 3   ENACTING THE ROLE OF MANAGER

SECTION 4   ENACTING THE ROLE OF CHANGE LEADER

SECTION 5   TOOLS FOR CONDUCTING MANAGEMENT AND CHANGE LEADERSHIP

◆   Introduction to the Tools Section

SECTION 6   AFTERWORD

SECTION 7   BIBLIOGRAPHY

Introduction to the Tools Section

This section presents two different tools:

♦ Figure 5.1, Worksheet to Guide the Management of WLP: Use this worksheet to guide you through the key questions to ask for effective management of WLP.

♦ Figure 5.2, Worksheet to Guide Change Leadership: Use this worksheet to guide you through the key questions to ask for effective change leadership.

Figure 5.1: Worksheet to Guide the Management of WLP

Directions: Use this tool to guide you from start to finish and step-by-step through managing the WLP function or effort. You do not have to use every question, and you may wish to add questions when appropriate. This tool is a template to guide your questioning as you manage a WLP department or project.

	Step 1: Formulate a Vision of WLP for the Organization, Department, or Work Group
1	Who should bear responsibility for WLP, and who should WLP primarily serve?
2	What should be the role of WLP in the organization, and why should it enact that role?
3	When should WLP be a key focus of attention in the organization, and why is that appropriate?
4	Where—that is, in what geographical locations or in what part of the organization—should WLP be centered?
5	Why should the organization sponsor WLP, and what results should be sought from it?

6	How should WLP be carried out in the organization?

7	How much should WLP contribute to the organization, and how should its results be assessed, tracked, and communicated?

Step 2: Communicate the Vision to Others and Build Their Enthusiasm

1	How can the vision of the WLP effort be most effectively communicated to key stakeholder groups inside and outside the organization?

2	How can the relative effectiveness of these communication strategies be assessed?

(continued on next page)

Figure 5.1: Worksheet to Guide the Management of WLP *(continued)*

Step 2: Communicate the Vision to Others and Build Their Enthusiasm *(continued)*

3 How can the reactions of key stakeholder groups to the vision be organized?

Step 3: Clarify the Goals and Objectives Necessary to Realize the Vision

1 Who are our customers and stakeholders, and what do they really need to improve their performance?

2 What philosophy should govern procedures for serving our customers and stakeholders?

3 When should customers be served? Should WLP strive to anticipate their needs, meet their needs as they surface, or meet needs after they are recognized?

4	Where should needs be met? On the job? Near the job? Off the job? What combination is best?
5	Why should the needs be met? What measurable outcomes can be forecast? How can costs and benefits of learning and nonlearning interventions be estimated?
6	How should needs be met? What learning and nonlearning interventions should be the special forte of the WLP effort? How are referrals made to other sources of assistance when necessary?

Step 4: Clarify the People, Data, and Things Necessary to Realize the Vision

1	How many and what kind of people are needed to achieve the goals and objectives of the WLP effort? How can they be justified on the basis of costs and benefits?

(continued on next page)

Step 4: Clarify the People, Data, and Things Necessary to Realize the Vision *(continued)*

2 How much and what kind of data are needed to achieve the goals and objectives of the WLP effort?

3 How much and what kind of things—including tools, equipment, and other objects, such as physical resources (buildings)—are needed to achieve the goals and objectives of the WLP effort?

Step 5: Create and Implement an Action Plan and Align It With Organizational and HR Plans

1 What performance problem or business issue gives rise to the need for the intervention? What is the estimated cost of the problem, and on what basis was that estimated cost determined?

2	What strategy for performance improvement is desirable to solve the problem or meet the business need? Why is that strategy preferable to obvious or cost-effective alternatives? What are the specific goals and objectives for the intervention?
3	How will the intervention or project be aligned with organizational plans? With HR plans?
4	How will the project be implemented? Through what step-by-step process will the project be undertaken? What outcomes or deliverables should be received from each step? How will the relative success of each step be measured? Who will be responsible for each step? What are the client's and consultant's responsibilities in each step?
5	What is the timeline for the project? How long will the project take to implement, and what steps will be undertaken when?
6	What is the budget for the project? What are the expected costs and benefits of the project?

(continued on next page)

Step 5: Create and Implement an Action Plan and Align It With Organizational and HR Plans *(continued)*

7 Who should participate in the project? What staff from inside and outside the organization will be necessary?

Step 6: Establish the Policy, Select and Develop People, Organize and Schedule Work Processes, Assign Responsibility, and Lead the Work

1 What policies for WLP does the organization need?

2 What policies for WLP may need to be changed as conditions affecting the organization change?

3 What kind and how many people are needed now to carry out the purpose and achieve the goals and objectives of the WLP effort?

4 What kind and how many people will be needed in the future to carry out the purpose and achieve the goals and objectives of the WLP effort?

5	How should people bearing WLP responsibilities be developed now and in the future?
6	How are work processes for WLP organized now? How should they be organized in the future?
7	How are work processes for WLP scheduled now? How should they be scheduled in the future?
8	How are work responsibilities for WLP assigned now? How should they be assigned in the future?
9	How are WLP staff members being led now? How should they be led in the future in ways that will encourage them to achieve the desired work results?

Step 7: Establish and Maintain a Work Climate That Is Conducive to Realizing the Vision and Implementing the Action Plan

1	What is the current climate of the WLP department or project? What should be the climate in the opinion of WLP staff members?

(continued on next page)

Figure 5.1: Worksheet to Guide the Management of WLP *(continued)*

Step 7: Establish and Maintain a Work Climate That Is Conducive to Realizing the Vision and Implementing the Action Plan *(continued)*

2	What barriers to performance or causes of dissatisfaction are evident among WLP staff? What causes them?
3	How can the barriers to performance or causes of dissatisfaction be addressed?

Step 8: Develop a Follow-Up and Monitoring System to Track Results Against Intentions

1	What approach will work best in the organization to provide follow-up and monitoring to stakeholders that will compare results to intentions?

2	Who needs information about the results of WLP, and what will they do with those results?
3	How can all relevant stakeholder groups use such a system?

Step 9: Establish and Implement a Communication Strategy and Plan to Build Enthusiasm for WLP Initiatives

1	Who should receive information about WLP efforts?
2	What kind of information should they receive?
3	When should the WLP effort or department communicate with others?

(continued on next page)

Figure 5.1: Worksheet to Guide the Management of WLP (continued)

Step 9: Establish and Implement a Communication Strategy and Plan to Build Enthusiasm for WLP Initiatives (continued)

4	Where should the WLP effort or department communicate with others?
5	Why should the WLP effort or department communicate?
6	How should the WLP effort or department communicate with others?

Step 10: Work With All Necessary Stakeholder Groups to Ensure Continuous Improvement of WLP Efforts

1	Who should be included in continuous improvement efforts for WLP in the organization?
2	What should be the focus of improvement for WLP?

3	When or how often should improvement efforts be undertaken for WLP?
4	Where (in what locations), if any, should continuous improvement efforts for WLP be focused?
5	What results should be tracked and monitored from continuous improvement efforts for WLP?
6	How should continuous improvement efforts for WLP efforts be undertaken?

Figure 5.2: Worksheet to Guide Change Leadership

Directions: Use this tool to guide you from start to finish and step-by-step through change leadership. You do not have to use every question, and you may wish to add questions when appropriate. This tool is a template to guide your questioning during change leadership.

Step 1: Identify the Stakeholders Who Stand to Gain From the Benefits of an Intervention

1 Who are the stakeholders who want or need information about the implementation or the progress of the intervention on a frequent basis?

2 What kind of information do the stakeholders prefer to receive?

3 How do the stakeholders prefer to receive information?

4	How often do the stakeholders prefer to receive information?

Step 2: Formulate a Strategy for Collecting the Results of the Intervention and Communicating Them to Key Stakeholders

1	What strategy will be most effective for communicating to stakeholders, on a continuing basis, about the intervention?

Step 3: Resolve Conflicts That Arise During Interventions

1	What conflicts are likely to arise before an intervention?

(continued on next page)

Figure 5.2: Worksheet to Guide Change Leadership *(continued)*

Step 3: Resolve Conflicts That Arise During Interventions *(continued)*

2	What conflicts are arising during the implementing of an intervention?
3	What is the nature of the conflict? From what cause or causes does it stem?
4	How many and what kinds of people are involved in, or are likely to be involved in, the conflict?
5	How destructive is the conflict? How constructive?

6 What strategies can be used by the change leader to focus attention on issues and goals and away from personalities?

7 What strategies are most effective in resolving conflict? How can stakeholders be trained on conflict resolution techniques so that they are equipped to diagnose and resolve their own conflicts?

Step 4: Communicate the Results to Excite Enthusiasm and Inspire Others About the Intervention

1 What are the key values of stakeholders?

(continued on next page)

Figure 5.2: Worksheet to Guide Change Leadership (continued)

Step 4: Communicate the Results to Excite Enthusiasm and Inspire Others About the Intervention (continued)

2	What results are different groups of stakeholders interested in, and why are they interested?
3	How can positive results of interventions be communicated in a way that will be most encouraging and motivating to stakeholders?
4	How can negative results of interventions be used to spur improvement efforts and avoid disappointment that is so keen that it demotivates improvement efforts?

SECTION 1   GETTING STARTED

SECTION 2   DEFINING THE ROLES

SECTION 3   ENACTING THE ROLE OF MANAGER

SECTION 4   ENACTING THE ROLE OF CHANGE LEADER

SECTION 5   TOOLS FOR CONDUCTING MANAGEMENT AND CHANGE LEADERSHIP

SECTION 6   AFTERWORD

- ◆ Why Is It Important to Master These Roles?
- ◆ How Does It Feel to Perform These Roles?
- ◆ What Should You Do Next?

SECTION 7   BIBLIOGRAPHY

This section addresses three key issues:

♦ Why is it important to master the roles of manager and change leader and the competencies associated with them?

♦ How does it feel to perform these roles?

♦ What should you do next?

Why Is It Important to Master These Roles?

The manager role oversees all others, and the change leader role guides people through interventions at the tactical level. The manager role overshadows all steps in the HPI process model, providing strategic guidance to all other roles. The change leader role occurs toward the end of the HPI process model and is closely associated with the work of the intervention implementor and evaluator. Without the manager role, WLP practitioners often would not have a strategic impact on their organizations and would be relegated to bit parts and minor roles. Without the change leader role, WLP practitioners would be more often asked for evidence that their work has had an impact on the organization and is worth the investments made in interventions.

The key to successful management of WLP is to find key leverage points in the organization that will yield the greatest impact on improved performance. That is as much an art as a science. Effective managers often find that management involves asking key stakeholders enough questions to find out the points of agreement about where the greatest benefit could be realized from an intervention and to break down the issues sufficiently enough to discern where, when, and how to intervene effectively.

The key to change leadership is to find successes resulting from interventions and to communicate that information to the stakeholders. That news heartens change participants and averts the criticism that often stems from lack of awareness of what happened as a result of interventions.

How Does It Feel to Perform These Roles?

Performing these roles requires as much intuition as analysis. *Intuition* is the ability to make good, quick,

and effective decisions when all the facts are not readily available or easily quantifiable.

Managers with WLP responsibilities must be able to pinpoint where WLP efforts will have the greatest impact, since resources such as time, money, and staff are scarce. Some organizations find that it is helpful to form triage teams, like those that set priorities in hospitals, to route requests for help to people who can analyze problems, determine causes, select interventions, design and develop interventions, implement the interventions, establish evaluation criteria, and track results. In this process, the manager with WLP responsibility is usually responsible for making the go–no-go decision as to whether a specific problem warrants the time and expense necessary to solve it. WLP managers are under pressure as never before to demonstrate the financial value of what they do and how their WLP departments perform. If they are not able to do that, then all or part of their department's responsibilities may be outsourced to private vendors or to local community colleges.

Change leaders serve in a role that decision makers and other stakeholders in organizations do not often appreciate enough. Whenever organizations implement major interventions, such as team-based management, customer service improvement, and business process reengineering, change leaders are needed to communicate the results of the intervention on a continuing basis and to help resolve conflicts stemming from differences in priorities and values. Many fine interventions have failed in execution because nobody was working on a tactical level every day with change sponsors, participants, and champions to ensure that results were identified, communicated, and used to motivate further action.

What Should You Do Next?

The Manager and the Change Leader is the fourth and final self-study job aid based on *ASTD Models for Workplace Learning and Performance* (Rothwell, Sanders, and Soper, 1999). Other volumes focus on other possible WLP roles, such as the analyst, evaluator, and intervention selector, intervention designer and developer, and intervention implementor. Use all the job aids to help build your competencies.

You might find it useful as well to refer to the tools found in section 5 of this volume to guide your daily application of the steps in demonstrating the competencies associated with the roles of manager of WLP and change leader. Finally, turn to section 7 for a comprehensive bibliography that can lead you to other publications to enhance your competencies in these areas.

SECTION 1   GETTING STARTED

SECTION 2   DEFINING THE ROLES

SECTION 3   ENACTING THE ROLE OF MANAGER

SECTION 4   ENACTING THE ROLE OF CHANGE LEADER

SECTION 5   TOOLS FOR CONDUCTING MANAGEMENT AND CHANGE LEADERSHIP

SECTION 6   AFTERWORD

SECTION 7   BIBLIOGRAPHY

Ackoff, R. (1993). "Idealized design: Creative corporate visioning." *Omega, 21*(4), 401–410.

Adler, K., and Swiercz, P. (1997). "Taming the performance bell curve." *Training & Development, 51*(10), 33–38.

Allen, E. (Ed.). (1990). *ASTD trainer's toolkit: Job descriptions in HRD.* Alexandria, VA: ASTD.

Allen, R. (1995). "On a clear day you can have a vision: A visioning model for everyone." *Leadership & Organization Development Journal, 16*(4), 39–44.

Anderson, D. (1998). "Aligned values + good job fit equals optimum performance." *National Productivity Review, 17*(4), 23–30.

Atkinson, V., and Chalmers, N. (1999). "Performance consulting: Get credit from your clients." *Performance Improvement, 38*(4), 14–19.

The best of managing the HRD function. (1992). Alexandria, VA: ASTD.

Blair, D., and Price, D. (1998). "Persistence: A key factor in human performance at work." *Performance Improvement, 37*(1), 27–31.

Bolman, L., and Deal, T. (1999). "Four steps to keeping change efforts heading in the right direction." *Journal for Quality and Participation, 22*(3), 6–11.

Bonner, D. (2000). "Enter the chief knowledge officer." *Training & Development, 54*(2), 36–40.

"Bringing Sears into the new world." (1997). *Fortune, 136*(7), 183–184.

Callahan, M. (1998). "The role of the performance evaluator." *Info-line.* No. 9803. Alexandria, VA: ASTD.

Carter, C. (1994). "Measuring and improving the human resources function." *Employment Relations Today, 21*(1), 63–75.

Chaston, I. (1993). "Performance improvement intervention: privatized and public sector organizations." *Leadership & Organization Development Journal, 14*(1), 4–8.

Dess, G., and Picken, J. (2000). "Changing roles: Leadership in the 21st century." *Organizational Dynamics, 28*(3), 18–33.

Dubois, D., and Rothwell, W. (1996a). *Developing the high-performance workplace: Administrator's handbook.* Amherst, MA: Human Resource Development.

Dubois, D., and Rothwell, W. (1996b). *Developing the high-performance workplace: Data collection instrument.* Amherst, MA: Human Resource Development.

Dubois, D., and Rothwell, W. (2000). *The competency toolkit.* (2 vols.). Amherst, MA: Human Resource Development.

Earl, M., and Scott, I. (1999). "What is a chief knowledge officer?" *Sloan Management Review, 40*(2), 29–38.

"The Few, the Proud—The Invisible? How to Develop Internal Consultants." (1998). *Training Directors Forum Newsletter, 14*(8), 1–4.

Finaly, J. (1994). "The Strategic Visioning Process." *Public Administration Quarterly, 18*(1), 64–74.

Frohman, A. (1997). "Igniting organizational change from below: The power of personal initiative." *Organizational Dynamics, 25*(3), 39–53.

Galpin, T. (1994). "How to manage human performance." *Employment Relations Today, 21*(2), 207–225.

George, S. (1997). "Focus through shared vision." *National Productivity Review, 16*(3), 65–74.

Gilley, J., Boughton, N., and Maycunich, A. (1999). *The performance challenge: Developing management systems to make employees your organization's greatest asset.* Reading, MA: Perseus.

Gilley, J., and Maycunich, A. (1998). *Strategically integrated HRD: Partnering to maximize organizational performance.* Reading, MA: Addison-Wesley.

Glanz, B. (1996). *Care packages for the workplace: Little things you can do to regenerate spirit at work.* New York: McGraw-Hill.

Grensing-Pophal, L. (2000). "Follow me." *HRMagazine, 45*(2), 36–41.

Hale, J. (1998). *The performance consultant's fieldbook.* San Francisco: Jossey-Bass.

Harvey, E. (1995). "Coaching for constant improvement." *Executive Excellence, 12*(7), 6.

Hawk, E. (1995). "Culture and rewards: A balancing act." *Personnel Journal, 74*(4), 30–37.

Hill, J., and Brethower, D. (1997). "Ridding ourselves of noninstruction." *Performance Improvement, 36*(8), 6–9.

Hooper, A. (1999). "Take it from the top." *People Management, 5*(16), 46–47, 49.

Horney, N., and Koonce, R. (1996). "Using competency alignment to shape, drive, and sustain change efforts." *National Productivity Review, 15*(3), 41–53.

Hutchinson, C., and Stein, F. (1998). "A whole new world of intervention: The performance technologist as integrating generalist." *Performance Improvement, 37*(5), 18–25.

Irvine, L. (1998, March-April). "Conflicts of interest." *British Journal of Administrative Management,* 8–10.

Kaplan, R., and Norton, D. (1996). *The balanced scorecard: Translating strategy into action.* Boston, MA: Harvard Business School.

Katzenbach, J. (1996). "New roads to job opportunity: From middle manager to real change leader." *Strategy & Leadership, 24*(4), 32–35.

Katzenbach, J., and the RCL Team. (1995). *Real change leaders: How you can create growth and high performance at your company.* New York: Times Business.

Kiser, A. (1998). *Masterful facilitation: Becoming a catalyst for meaningful change.* New York: AMACOM.

Klunk, S. (1997). "Conflict and the dynamic organization." *Hospital Materiel Management Quarterly, 19*(2), 37–44.

Koehle, D. (1999). "The role of the performance change manager." *Info-line.* No. 9715. Alexandria, VA: ASTD.

Kotter, J. (1999). "Change leadership." *Executive Excellence, 16*(4), 16–17.

Langdon, D. (2000). "Aligning performance: The ultimate goal of our profession." *Performance Improvement, 39*(3), 22–26.

Latham, J. (1995). "Visioning: The concept, trilogy, and process." *Quality Progress, 28*(4), 65–68.

Lee, C. (1993, February). "The vision thing." *Training,* 25–34.

Lingle, J.H., and Schiemann, W.A. (1996). "From balanced scorecard to strategic gauges: Is measurement worth it?" *Management Review, 85*(3), 56–61.

Manzoni, J., and Barsoux, J. (1998). "The set-up-to-fail syndrome." *Harvard Business Review, 76*(2), 101–113.

Markus, M., and Benjamin, R. (1997). "The magic bullet theory in IT—enabled transformation." *Sloan Management Review, 38*(2), 55–68.

Marsh, L. (1992). "Good manager: Good coach?— What is needed for effective coaching?" *Industrial & Commercial Training, 24*(9), 3–8.

Meister, J. (1998). "Ten steps to creating a corporate university." *Training & Development, 52*(11), 38–43.

Olivetti, L. (Ed.). (1990). *ASTD trainer's toolkit: Mission statements for HRD.* Alexandria, VA: ASTD.

Ray, R. (1997). "Developing internal consultants." *Training & Development, 51*(7), 30–34.

Rothwell, W. (2000). *The evaluator.* Alexandria, VA: ASTD.

Rothwell, W. (1996). "Selecting and developing the professional HRD staff." In R. Craig (Ed.), *Training and Development Handbook* (4th ed.). New York: McGraw-Hill.

Rothwell, W., and Kazanas, H. (1994a). *Human resource development: A strategic approach* (rev. edition). Amherst, MA: Human Resource Development.

Rothwell, W., and Kazanas, H. (1994b). *Planning and managing human resources: Strategic planning for personnel management* (rev. edition). Amherst, MA: Human Resource Development.

Rothwell, W., Prescott, R., and Taylor, M. (1998). *Strategic human resource leader: How to help your organization manage the six trends affecting the workforce.* Palo Alto, CA: Davies-Black.

Rothwell, W., Sanders, E., and Soper, J. (1999). *ASTD models for workplace learning and performance: Roles, competencies, and outputs.* Alexandria, VA: ASTD.

Rothwell, W., and Sredl, H. (2000). *The ASTD reference guide to workplace learning and performance* (3rd ed., 2 vols.). Amherst, MA: Human Resource Development.

Rothwell, W., Sullivan, R., and McLean, G. (Eds.). (1995). *Practicing organization development: A guide for consultants.* San Francisco: Jossey-Bass/Pfeiffer.

Russo, E. (1997). "Change leadership." *Executive Excellence, 14*(10), 12.

Rye, D. (1998). *1,001 ways to inspire: Your organization, your team, and yourself.* Franklin Lakes, NJ: Career Press.

Saunier, A., and Mavis, M. (1998). "Fixing a broken system." *HRfocus, 75*(3), 1, 3–4.

Schermerhorn, J., Gardner, W., and Martin, T. (1990). "Management dialogues: Turning on the marginal performer." *Organizational Dynamics, 18*(4), 47–59.

Schneider, D., and Goldwasser, C. (1998). "Be a model leader of change." *Management Review, 87*(3), 41–45.

Sensenig, K. (1998). A Single-Site Descriptive Analysis of Managers' Perceptions Concerning the Value-Added of Linking Leadership Development Efforts to Strategic Corporate Objectives. Unpublished Ph.D. dissertation. University Park: Pennsylvania State University.

Sharpe, C. (1998). *The Info-line guide to performance improvement.* Alexandria, VA: ASTD.

Shelton, C. (1999). *Quantum leaps: 7 skills for workplace recreation.* Boston: Butterworth-Heinemann.

Sherman, S. (1995). "Company change agents." *Fortune, 132*(12), 197–198.

Sherriton, J., and Stern, J. (1997). "HR's role in culture change." *HRFocus, 74*(4), 27.

Smith, D. (1998). "Invigorating change initiatives." *Management Review, 87*(5), 45–48.

Spitzer, D. (1996). "Ensuring successful performance improvement interventions." *Performance Improvement, 35*(9), 26–27.

Spurling, M., and Trolley, E. (2000). "How to make training strategic." *People Management, 6*(8), 46–48.

Stadius, R. (Ed.). (1999). *ASTD trainer's toolkit: job descriptions in workplace learning and performance.* Alexandria, VA: ASTD.

Swanson, R., and Holton, E. (1998). "Developing and maintaining core expertise in the midst of change." *National Productivity Review, 17*(2), 29–38.

Tamir, L. (1999). "Conflict mediation." *Executive Excellence, 16*(6), 15–16.

Taylor, D. (Ed.). (1998). *Managing the small training staff.* Alexandria, VA: ASTD.

Thorlakson, A. (1997). "Performance improvement counselling." *Canadian Manager, 22*(4), 16, 26.

Tosti, D., and Jackson, S. (1994). "Alignment: How it works and why it matters." *Training, 31*(4), 58–64.

Ulrich, D. (1997). *Human resource champions: The next agenda for adding value and delivering results.* Boston: Harvard Business School.

Whiteside, K. (1997). "Implementing performance interventions." *Performance Improvement, 36*(10), 6–10.

Wilburn, K., and Wilburn, H. (1998). "Eleven techniques to jump-start performance dialogue." *Performance Improvement, 37*(1), 24–26.

Willis, V. (1991). "The new learning organization: Should there be a chief learning officer in the house?" *Human Resource Development Quarterly, 2*(2), 181–187.

Younger, S. (1999). "How to develop a vision." *Info-line.* No. 9107. Alexandria, VA: ASTD.

Zemke, R. (1996). "The call of community." *Training, 33*(3), 24–30.